FIFA 23

The Complete Guide & Walkthrough with
Tips &Tricks

FIFA 23 Guide: FUT 23 Walkthrough, Tips, Tricks, and How to Win More Matches

FIFA 23 is the latest in EA Sports' long-running football franchise, developed by EA Canada. The soccer simulation depicts the 2022-2023 season across many of the world's best leagues, including the Premier League, Bundesliga, and La Liga. It also includes a number of licensed competitions, like the UEFA Champions League and UEFA Europa League, as well as the upcoming FIFA World Cup Qatar 2022 and FIFA Women's World Cup Australia/New Zealand 2023.

Spanning a variety of modes, including Career, Ultimate Team, Volta Football, and Pro Clubs, in this FIFA 23 guide we're going to share our Tips and Tricks for How to Win More Matches. We'll show you how to get started in our FUT 23 walkthrough, and reveal the Best Formations and Custom Tactics for FUT. And don't worry if you're more of a single player fan, because we've got you covered with the Best Hidden Gems in Career Mode and much more.

Please note there are some minor differences between the PS5 and PS4 versions of the game which may lead to some inconsistencies in our instructions.

 On this page:

FIFA 23 Guide: FUT 23 Walkthrough

FIFA 23 Guide: Career Mode

FIFA 23 Guide: FUT 23 Walkthrough

FIFA 23 Ultimate Team, or FUT 23 as it's also known, is the flagship mode in FIFA 23, where you're tasked with collecting Players in order to assemble teams of superstars from both the past and present. Chemistry is a key mechanic which buffs the attributes of Players, if they're lined up in the same squad as teammates of the same nationality, league, or real-world team. In this part of our FIFA 23 guide, we'll help you to build an unstoppable Ultimate Team and show you how to win more matches in modes like FUT Champions and FUT Rivals.

FIFA 23: Best Formations and Custom Tactics for FUT

Looking for the best formations and custom tactics for FUT in FIFA 23? FUT 23, or FIFA Ultimate Team, sees you assembling a squad of football superstars, both past and present, from a variety of clubs and leagues around the world. But before you can even begin to think about Players and Chemistry, you're probably going to want to determine the best formations and custom tactics for your team. This is because your formation will ultimately determine the type of positions you need to fill, while also affecting your approach on the pitch. As part of our FIFA 23 guide, we're going to share the best formations and custom tactics for FUT, including meta formations.

On this page:

FIFA 23 Guide: FUT 23 Walkthrough

FIFA 23 Ultimate Team, or FUT 23 as it's also known, is the flagship mode in FIFA 23, where you're tasked with collecting Players in order to assemble teams of superstars from both the past and present. Chemistry is a key mechanic which buffs the attributes of Players, if they're lined up in the same squad as teammates of the same nationality, league, or real-world team. In this part of our FIFA 23 guide, we'll help you to build an unstoppable Ultimate Team and show you how to win more matches in modes like FUT Champions and FUT Rivals.

FIFA 23: Best Formations and Custom Tactics for FUT

Looking for the best formations and custom tactics for FUT in FIFA 23? FUT 23, or FIFA Ultimate Team, sees you assembling a squad of football superstars, both past and present, from a variety of clubs and leagues around the world. But before you can even begin to think about Players and Chemistry, you're probably going to want to determine the best formations and custom tactics for your team. This is because your formation will ultimately determine the type of positions you need to fill, while also affecting your approach on the pitch. As part of our FIFA 23 guide, we're going to share the best formations and custom tactics for FUT, including meta formations.

 On this page:

FIFA 23: Best Formations and Custom Tactics for FUT

The best formations for FUT in FIFA 23 will depend a lot on the Players you have available and exactly how you want to play on the pitch.

If you're more a defensive player then you may want to consider going with a back five, which will help to prevent teams from scoring against you at the expense of you being able to effectively attack.

Alternatively, you may prefer the even distribution of players that a 4-4-2 provides, giving you a stable rear-guard with enough midfielders to get the ball into your forwards.

It's always important to consider Chemistry: FIFA 23 is much more flexible on this front, but you should still carefully plan how to bring together all of your best players into a formidable starting eleven.

For example, if you have two top-notch strikers in your team, you may want to find a way to accommodate both of them, rather than stick one on the bench. You can change the position of players using Position Items to retain good Chemistry.

Even if you don't necessarily have many great Players in your team yet, picking a formation can help you develop the kind of squad you want.

Once you've settled on a structure and tactics for your team, then you can begin to think about the type of personnel you'll need to get the most out of it.

Does your starting eleven rely on rapid wingbacks, shuttling up-and-down either side of the field? Or do you need a target man, capable of bringing the ball under control and facilitating attacking teammates? Selecting the best formations for FUT can really help give you a foundation to build from.

Remember, this article exists to give you inspiration and ideas, but is not necessarily definitive.

While there are often meta formations in competitive games like FIFA 23, you should experiment and find the best formations and custom tactics that work for you and your Players.

Don't be afraid to try out different line-ups and explore all of the different tools that the game gives you. We'd also like to add that, while this page has been written with FIFA Ultimate Team, or FUT 23, in mind, a lot of the same strategies and concepts apply to Career Mode as well.

4-4-2

The foundation of English football, the 4-4-2, is a rock solid option in FIFA 23, and probably the best formation for you to get your feet wet in FUT 23. This year's game is slower and more deliberate, so it actually pays to play it a little safe and go back to basics in many ways.

The goal with this formation is to have two central midfielders building a base in central midfield, with two overlapping fullbacks covered by a couple of wingers who are willing to get back on defense. We like to ensure our forwards stay central, but it's good to have one pacey workhorse who helps out in defence and is also willing to run in behind, and then partner him with a second forward who stays forward and can hold up the ball.

Winning the ball back high up the pitch can also be effective with this formation, and as this year's game allows for five substitutions, you don't need to worry too much about running out of stamina — as long, of course, as you have a strong bench. Obviously, you may want to tone down your tactics if you want to conserve energy, but this is up to you.

4-4-2 Custom Tactics and Instructions

As alluded to above, your Defensive Style is going to be determined by how gung-ho you feel with regards to winning the ball back. Personally, we're having success with Press After Possession Loss, but this is a stamina hog, so that's something to keep in mind. If you want to be a lot more conservative, you could look at the 4-4-2 Holding formation as an alternative to simply sit off opponents and block off their passing lanes. Even with the traditional 4-4-2, we'd still recommend you play Long Ball to setup those counter attacks. Remember, if you lose possession and you are going to press immediately, keep your Depth quite high to really try and win the ball high up the pitch. However, if you feel you're getting caught out a lot, feel free to drop off.

Ideally, you'll want your CMs to Cover Center to provide that foundation in the middle of the pitch, but instruct your fullbacks to Overlap to provide additional attacking potency when you're on the offensive. Instructing your wingers to Come Back on Defence can help plug any gaps. We like having a pacier striker to both Get in Behind and Come Back on Defence, while leaving a target man on Stay Forward to help pick up Long Balls and hold up the play.

Defence

Defensive Style: Press After Possession Loss or Balanced

Width: 60

Depth: 55

Offence

Build Up Play: Long Ball

Chance Creation: Balanced or Direct Passing

Width: 50

Players in Box: 6

Corners: 2

Free Kicks: 2

Here are some Instructions for your Players that you may want to consider based on the information above. The key thing is that your CMs build a base for everything that you do, and your fullbacks supplement the attack while still receiving defensive support from your wingers.

Position	Instructions
GK	Saving on Crosses: Balanced Saving Outside Box: Balanced
LB	Attacking Runs: Stay Back While Attacking Interceptions: Conservative Interceptions Run Type: Overlap Defensive Position: Stick to Position
Left CB	Attacking Support: Stay Back While Attacking Interceptions: Normal Interceptions Defensive Position: Stick to Position
Right CB	Attacking Support: Stay Back While Attacking Interceptions: Normal Interceptions Defensive Position: Stick to Position
RB	Attacking Runs: Stay Back While Attacking Interceptions: Conservative Interceptions Run Type: Overlap Defensive Position: Stick to Position
LM	Defensive Support: Come Back on Defence Chance Creation: Balance Width

Position	Instructions
	Support Runs: Get in Behind
	Support on Crosses: Get into the Box for Cross
	Interceptions: Normal Interceptions
Left CM	Attacking Support: Balanced Attack or Stay Back While Attacking
	Support on Crosses: Get into the Box for Cross or Stay on Edge of Box for Cross
	Interceptions: Normal Interceptions
	Defensive Position: Cover Centre
	Positioning Freedom: Stick to Position
Right CM	Attacking Support: Balanced Attack or Stay Back While Attacking
	Support on Crosses: Get into the Box for Cross or Stay on Edge of Box for Cross
	Interceptions: Normal Interceptions
	Defensive Position: Cover Centre
	Positioning Freedom: Stick to Position
RM	Defensive Support: Come Back on Defence
	Chance Creation: Balance Width
	Support Runs: Get in Behind
	Support on Crosses: Get into the Box for Cross
	Interceptions: Normal Interceptions
Left ST	Support Runs: Stay Central

Position	Instructions
	Attacking Runs: Get in Behind or Mixed Attack
	Interceptions: Normal Interceptions
	Defensive Support: Come Back on Defence or Stay Forward
	Support Runs: Stay Central
Right ST	Attacking Runs: Get in Behind or Mixed Attack
	Interceptions: Normal Interceptions
	Defensive Support: Come Back on Defence or Stay Forward

4-2-3-1

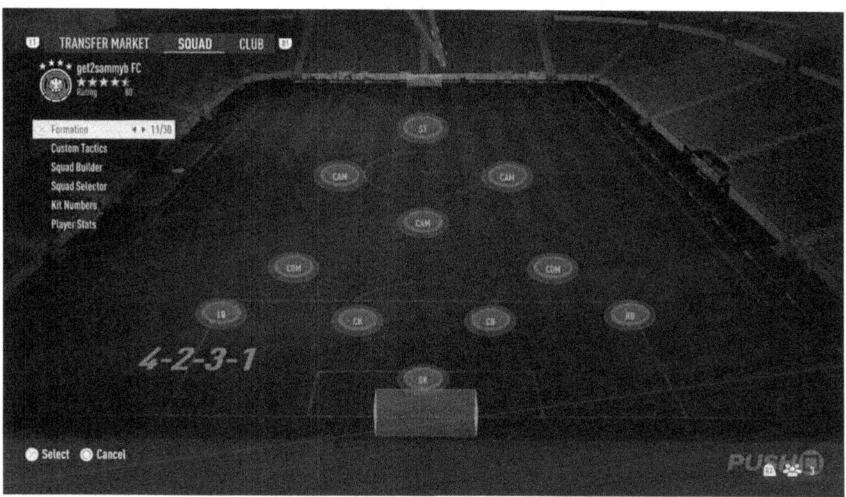

Formation	Pros	Cons
4-2-3-1	A great foundation formation that you can use at the beginning of games or when you've built up a	Can lack width without energetic fullbacks.

Formation	Pros	Cons
	lead and are looking to steadily see out the remainder of a game. Impressive defensive cover from CDMs who can help to shield your centre backs and protect your backline.	Requires attacking midfielders to get in the box and make runs in order to support lone striker.

If you're struggling to shut out opponents in FIFA 23, then the 4-2-3-1 can be a great formation to utilise in order to give you a lot of defensive stability. Due to the way the game's designed, you're going to get a lot of support from your CDM players, who will shield your back four, assuming you've got your Custom Tactics assigned appropriately. This makes it a great formation to start out in or to switch to when you have a lead or are comfortably in front.

The downside is that you may not get much width from your attacking midfielders operating behind the striker, but you can offset this by using energetic fullbacks who can get up and down the pitch. Remember, you'll still have those two CDMs in front of your back four who can help you to mop up any potential counter-attacks should the situation arise. Alternatively, you can opt for the 4-2-3-1 Wide formation, which will give you a bit more width at the expense of some stability in the centre of the park.

Perhaps the only problem with this formation is that it can feel a little toothless in attack at times, but again you can offset this by encouraging your attacking midfielders to push forward or even hold their position up the field, helping you to break out more easily. Given how potent crossing can be, you're going to want to instruct your wide attacking midfielders to get into the box, giving you options from your striker both in front of goal and at the far posts.

4-2-3-1 Custom Tactics and Instructions

There's one major decision you'll need to make with your Custom Tactics for the 4-2-3-1: how defensive do you want to be? If you're primarily looking for stability at the back, then we'd recommend you keep your fullbacks in position during offensive possessions, and the same with your CDMs as well. If you're looking for a little more offensive potency, then you can put your fullbacks' Attacking Runs to Balanced, and even instruct one of your CDMs to get forward during attacks. If you do adopt these kind of tactics, however, make sure the other CDM stays back to give you some insurance.

Here are some of the Custom Tactics you should consider for the 4-2-3-1 formation. You can also tinker with the offensive width if you're looking to spray the ball about more, but do keep in mind that this will leave some gaps in the centre of the park if you do lose possession:

Defence

Defensive Style: Balanced

Width: 50

Depth: 50

Offence

Build Up Play: Slow Build Up

Chance Creation: Forward Runs or Balanced

Width: 60

Players in Box: 5

Corners: 2

Free Kicks: 2

In addition, here are some Instructions for your Players that you may want to adopt as a starting point for the 4-2-3-1 formation. As always, feel free to play around with these Instructions and see what works best for your personal playstyle. As mentioned above, a lot of this will depend on how defensive or offensive you want to be:

Position	Instructions
GK	Saving on Crosses: Balanced Saving Outside Box: Balanced

Position	Instructions
LB	Attacking Runs: Balanced or Stay Back in Attack Interceptions: Normal Interceptions Run Type: Mixed Attack Defensive Position: Stick to Position
Left CB	Attacking Support: Stay Back While Attacking Interceptions: Normal Interceptions Defensive Position: Stick to Position
Right CB	Attacking Support: Stay Back While Attacking Interceptions: Normal Interceptions Defensive Position: Stick to Position
RB	Attacking Runs: Balanced or Stay Back in Attack Interceptions: Normal Interceptions Run Type: Mixed Attack Defensive Position: Stick to Position
Left CDM	Defensive Behaviour: Balanced Defence Attacking Support: Balanced Attack or Stay Back While Attacking Interceptions: Normal Interceptions Defensive Position: Cover Centre Positioning Freedom: Stick to Position

Position	Instructions
Right CDM	Defensive Behaviour: Balanced Defence
	Attacking Support: Balanced Attack or Stay Back While Attacking
	Interceptions: Normal Interceptions
	Defensive Position: Cover Centre
	Positioning Freedom: Stick to Position
Left CAM	Defensive Support: Basic Defence Support
	Support on Crosses: Get into the Box for Cross
	Positioning Freedom: Stick to Position
	Interceptions: Normal Interceptions
Centre CAM	Defensive Support: Basic Defence Support
	Support on Crosses: Balanced Crossing Runs
	Positioning Freedom: Stick to Position
	Interceptions: Normal Interceptions
Right CAM	Defensive Support: Basic Defence Support
	Support on Crosses: Get into the Box for Cross
	Positioning Freedom: Stick to Position
	Interceptions: Normal Interceptions
ST	Support Runs: Balanced Width
	Attacking Runs: Mixed Attack
	Interceptions: Normal Interceptions

Position	Instructions
Defensive Support:	Stay Forward

4-4-2 Holding

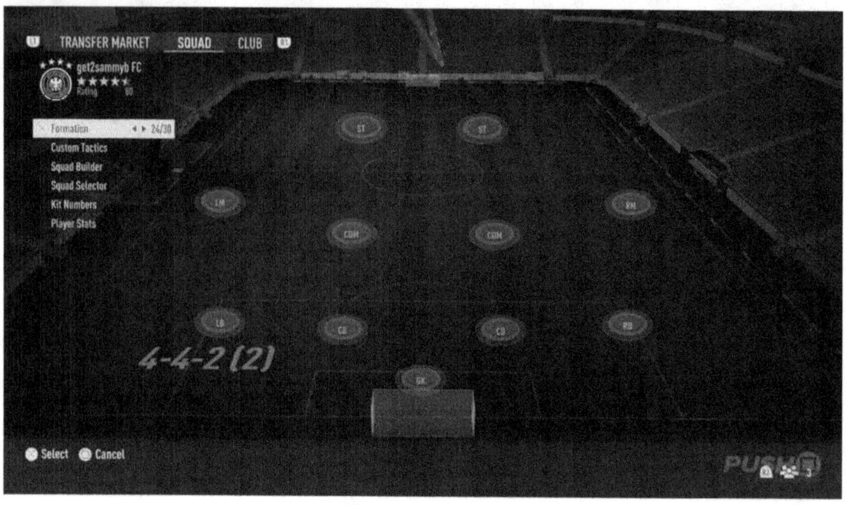

Formation	Pros	Cons
4-4-2 Holding	Tons of defensive stability provided by the two CDMs in the centre of the park.	Can be a little too conservative and overrun in midfield, leaving forwards isolated and wide players ineffective.
	Wide midfielders can effectively overlap, creating overloads in attack.	
	A balanced and flexible formation that has no real weaknesses to expose.	

While the 4-4-2 may be quite old-fashioned in the modern game, the 4-4-2 Holding formation is brilliantly balanced and gives you versatility in both defence and attack. While this is unquestionably a more conservative formation, with its second bank of four anchored by two CDMs, if you can use your wide midfielders to stretch the pitch it can be deadly offensively while still commanding more than enough defensive stability to avoid ceding easy opportunities to your opponent.

You're probably going to want to instruct your fullbacks to stay back, especially if you've got your wide midfielders pushing forward to complement your attack, but you should have more than enough defensive cover from your CDMs to break up any potential counter-attacks.

There are a number of permutations of the 4-4-2 you could experiment with, including the 4-2-2-2 which is a lot more offensively minded at the expense of width. This alternative can be a little narrow and so will rely on your fullbacks providing options out wide, but it's flexible and with a couple of creative CAMs up front will result in a ton of goal scoring potential if you prefer to build up slowly and play through the middle.

4-4-2 Holding Custom Tactics and Instructions

The conventional 4-4-2 is quite adaptable, meaning that you can make it as offensive or defensive as you like with your Custom Tactics. But if you're opting for the 4-4-2 Holding then there's a good chance you're looking to keep it tight at the back. Defensively, you should be pretty safe, but getting the ball up the pitch when in possession can be quite laboured, so we'd recommend opting for Long Ball as your Build Up Play style.

If you feel you're not getting enough options upfront, even with the two strikers, then you can instruct your LM and RM players to Cut Inside, but you will lose width this way and may have to instruct your LB and RB to Overlap in order to offset it. Just be warned that this will leave you exposed in wide areas, and if you're up against an opponent who has pacey wingers then they will punish you. We'd recommend you instruct your fullbacks to hold their position during attacks, and try to rely on the natural width that your wide midfielders provide:

Defence

Defensive Style: Balanced

Width: 50

Depth: 50

Offence

Build Up Play: Long Ball

Chance Creation: Balanced

Width: 55

Players in Box: 5

Corners: 2

Free Kicks: 2

With all that in mind, here are some Instructions for your Players that you may want to tinker with if you're planning to use the 4-4-2 Holding formation. As discussed already, you should mess with these Instructions and see what works best for your personal playstyle. We'd always recommend starting out with Balanced on everything and then tinkering to your tastes. With the CDMs, you can allow the more offensive minded player to stray forward, as long as you keep one to Stay Back While Attacking:

Position	Instructions
GK	Saving on Crosses: Balanced Saving Outside Box: Balanced
LB	Attacking Runs: Stay Back While Attacking Interceptions: Normal Interceptions Run Type: Mixed Attack Defensive Position: Stick to Position
Left CB	Attacking Support: Stay Back While Attacking Interceptions: Normal Interceptions Defensive Position: Stick to Position
Right CB	Attacking Support: Stay Back While Attacking

Position	Instructions
	Interceptions: Normal Interceptions Defensive Position: Stick to Position
RB	Attacking Runs: Stay Back While Attacking Interceptions: Normal Interceptions Run Type: Mixed Attack Defensive Position: Stick to Position
LM	Defensive Support: Basic Defence Support Chance Creation: Balance Width Support Runs: Balanced Support Support on Crosses: Balanced Crossing Runs Interceptions: Normal Interceptions
Left CDM	Defensive Behaviour: Balanced Defence Attacking Support: Balanced Attack or Stay Back While Attacking Interceptions: Normal Interceptions Defensive Position: Cover Centre Positioning Freedom: Stick to Position
Right CDM	Defensive Behaviour: Balanced Defence Attacking Support: Balanced Attack or Stay Back While Attacking Interceptions: Normal Interceptions Defensive Position: Cover Centre Positioning Freedom: Stick to Position

Position	Instructions
RM	Defensive Support: Basic Defence Support Chance Creation: Balance Width Support Runs: Balanced Support Support on Crosses: Balanced Crossing Runs Interceptions: Normal Interceptions
Left ST	Support Runs: Balanced Width Attacking Runs: Mixed Attack Interceptions: Normal Interceptions Defensive Support: Basic Defence Support
Right ST	Support Runs: Balanced Width Attacking Runs: Mixed Attack Interceptions: Normal Interceptions Defensive Support: Basic Defence Support

4-1-2-1-2 Narrow

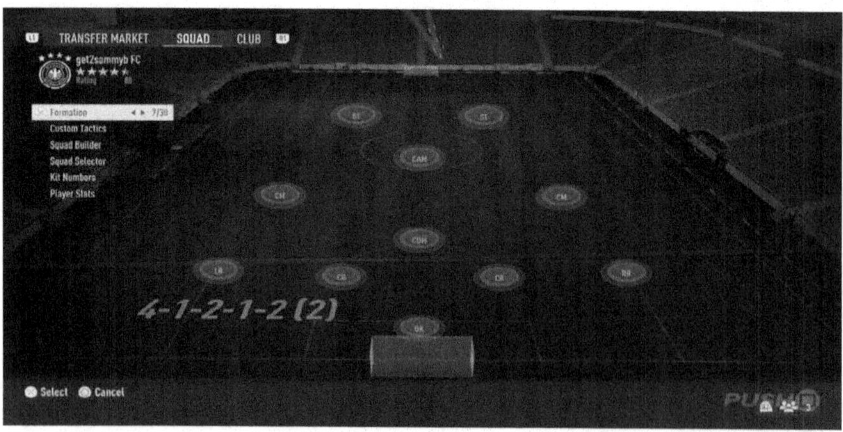

Formation	Pros	Cons
4-1-2-1-2 Narrow	Robust in the centre of the park, with plenty of attacking options and defensive coverage. Two striker formation with a CAM feeding them is difficult for defenders to track and can cause overloads.	Narrow formation can get exposed on the counter-attack. Not much width in attacking areas to feed forwards.

The 4-1-2-1-2 Narrow is one of the best formations for FUT because it offers a robust central midfield with excellent attacking options and plenty of defensive coverage.

With the two strikers upfront and the CAM feeding them from slightly deeper areas, this favours the Forward Runs command for Chance Creation and can overload defences, particularly on the counter-attack. It does, however, lack a bit of width in the outside areas. You can counter this by opting for the 4-1-2-1-2 Wide formation, but this stretches the pitch and leaves space to exploit in the centre of the field.

If you do opt for the 4-1-2-1-2 Narrow, then you're going to need two very good fullbacks who are capable of shuttling up and down the pitch when called upon. We'd recommend instructing the more attacking of the duo to push forward with Balanced Attacks where possible, while assigning the more defensively minded player to Stay Back While Attacking. This will just give you a little more insurance should you get countered on.

You're going to need a bit of Width in both defence and offence, just to prevent players from stepping on each others' toes. The really good thing about this formation is that you can easily switch to a 4-2-3-1 if you need a little more defensive stability at any point, or even a 4-4-2 depending on your available personnel.

4-1-2-1-2 Narrow Custom Tactics and Instructions

The 4-1-2-1-2 Narrow isn't massively adaptable, as your Custom Tactics are likely going to rely on your CDM being assigned to Stay Back While Attacking and your CAM to Stay Forward so that your strikers don't get isolated. We'd recommend you keep your strikers up the pitch, allowing your CAM to feed them as they make Forward Runs into the box.

It makes sense to have one CM assigned to Balanced Attack and the other to Get Forward, giving you a little more stability in the middle of the park should you lose possession while still having plenty of attacking options when you're in possession of the ball. You could also try Fast Build Up play if you prefer to move the ball about swiftly in possession:

Defence

Defensive Style: Balanced

Width: 50

Depth: 60

Offence

Build Up Play: Balanced

Chance Creation: Forward Runs

Width: 50

Players in Box: 5

Corners: 2

Free Kicks: 2

We've included some example Instructions for your Players in the 4-1-2-1-2 Narrow formation below, but as always these are just a starting point for you to tinker with. Consider how offensive or defensive you'd like to play, and tweak the settings to your tastes. For example, if you find you're getting exposed on the wings, then you're going to need to sacrifice width by setting your fullbacks to Stay Back While Attacking:

Position	Instructions
GK	Saving on Crosses: Balanced Saving Outside Box: Balanced

Position	Instructions
LB	Attacking Runs: Balanced Attack or Stay Back While Attacking
	Interceptions: Normal Interceptions
	Run Type: Mixed Attack
	Defensive Position: Stick to Position
Left CB	Attacking Support: Stay Back While Attacking
	Interceptions: Normal Interceptions
	Defensive Position: Stick to Position
Right CB	Attacking Support: Stay Back While Attacking
	Interceptions: Normal Interceptions
	Defensive Position: Stick to Position
RB	Attacking Runs: Balanced Attack or Stay Back While Attacking
	Interceptions: Normal Interceptions
	Run Type: Mixed Attack
	Defensive Position: Stick to Position
CDM	Defensive Behaviour: Balanced Defence
	Attacking Support: Stay Back While Attacking
	Interceptions: Normal Interceptions
	Defensive Position: Cover Centre
	Positioning Freedom: Stick to Position
Left CM	Attacking Support: Balanced Attack or Get Forward

Position	Instructions
	Support on Crosses: Balanced Crossing Runs
	Interceptions: Normal Interceptions
	Positioning Freedom: Stick to Position
	Defensive Position: Cover Wing
Right CM	Attacking Support: Balanced Attack or Get Forward
	Support on Crosses: Balanced Crossing Runs
	Interceptions: Normal Interceptions
	Positioning Freedom: Stick to Position
	Defensive Position: Cover Wing
CAM	Defensive Support: Stay Forward
	Support on Crosses: Balanced Crossing Runs
	Positioning Freedom: Stick to Position
	Interceptions: Normal Interceptions
Left ST	Support Runs: Balanced Width
	Attacking Runs: Mixed Attack or Target Man
	Interceptions: Normal Interceptions
	Defensive Support: Basic Defence Support or Stay Forward
Right ST	Support Runs: Balanced Width
	Attacking Runs: Mixed Attack or Target Man
	Interceptions: Normal Interceptions
	Defensive Support: Basic Defence Support or Stay Forward

4-3-1-2

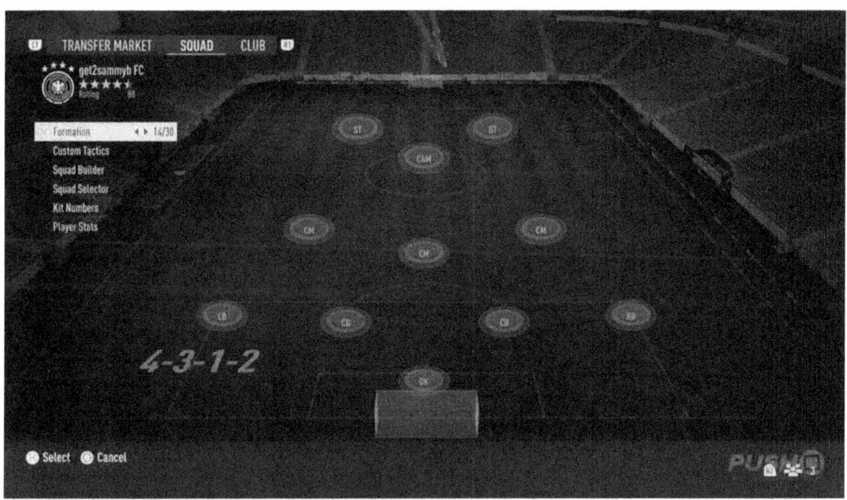

Formation	Pros	Cons
4-3-1-2	Compact in the middle of the park making it perfect for a possession-based game. Extremely attacking, with midfielders who can push forward and a CAM feeding two strikers upfront. Can effectively press from the front and pressure opponents into making mistakes and ceding possession high up the field.	Susceptible to being exposed by pacey wingers, especially if fullbacks push forward to provide attacking width. Can be a bit too narrow, and not much defensive cover if midfielders are assigned to assist in attack.

The 4-3-1-2 is compact in the middle and allows you to play a possession-based game, using your fullbacks to provide width in both offensive and defensive areas. This formation is effective at flooding the midfield, meaning that it can be used to foil to formations like 4-4-2, although it relies on energetic fullbacks who will need to shuttle up-and-down the field.

The downside is that longballs into the channels can leave you completely and utterly exposed, particularly against pacey players in wide areas. However, with two strikers upfront and a CAM feeding them, you'll be able to apply pressure in the final third consistently, pressing opponents into mistakes and effectively operating under the conditions of "offence is the best defence".

If this formation isn't attacking enough, then you could also try a 4-3-2-1, leaving your striker up the field at all times and instructing your CAMs to run in behind when in possession. Alternatively, you could try 4-3-3 Attack, which will give you a bit more width and spreads your personnel evenly across the two attacking thirds. The downside to all of these is that there's not a great deal of defensive stability, depending on how you set them up, so you'll likely be looking to outscore your opponents if you opt for them.

4-3-1-2 Custom Tactics and Instructions

As with any formation in FIFA 23, you can make the 4-3-1-2 work how you want it to, whether it's a defensive or offensive approach. However, your Custom Tactics for this formation are likely going to focus on possession-based play, as you're going to want to use your overloads in midfield to knock the ball around. Similarly, while you can instruct your fullbacks to Stay Back While Attacking for defensive insurance, you're basically going to have no width so will probably want them to Overlap.

Because of how possession focused this formation is, we'd recommend you choose Slow Build Up and even Possession-based Chance Creation. You can do Forward Runs if you're chasing the game, but with two strikers assigned to Get Behind you should have more than enough opportunity to penetrate your opposition's lines.

With your CMs, there's absolutely loads you can do: we'd recommend you instruct one to Stay Back While Attacking, then put the other two on Balanced. If you're worried you're not getting enough attacking support, then you can assign one of your other two CMs to Get Forward, but you probably shouldn't use this approach unless you need a goal.

Defence

Defensive Style: Balanced

Width: 55

Depth: 50

Offence

Build Up Play: Slow Build Up

Chance Creation: Possession

Width: 55

Players in Box: 4

Corners: 2

Free Kicks: 2

Below are some example Instructions for the 4-3-1-2 that you may want to consider implementing if you're planning to use this formation. Remember that you should tweak it to your tastes, depending on what Players you're using and what you're trying to achieve on the pitch. These are just starting points for you to experiment with and find what works for your playstyle:

Position	Instructions
GK	Saving on Crosses: Balanced Saving Outside Box: Balanced
LB	Attacking Runs: Balanced Attack Interceptions: Normal Interceptions Run Type: Overlap Defensive Position: Stick to Position
Left CB	Attacking Support: Stay Back While Attacking Interceptions: Normal Interceptions Defensive Position: Stick to Position
Right CB	Attacking Support: Stay Back While Attacking

Position	Instructions
	Interceptions: Normal Interceptions Defensive Position: Stick to Position
RB	Attacking Runs: Balanced Attack Interceptions: Normal Interceptions Run Type: Overlap Defensive Position: Stick to Position
Left CM	Attacking Support: Balanced Attack or Get Forward Support on Crosses: Balanced Crossing Runs Interceptions: Normal Interceptions Positioning Freedom: Stick to Position Defensive Position: Cover Centre
Centre CM	Attacking Support: Stay Back While Attacking Support on Crosses: Balanced Interceptions: Normal Interceptions Positioning Freedom: Stick to Position Defensive Position: Cover Centre
Right CM	Attacking Support: Balanced Attack or Get Forward Support on Crosses: Balanced Crossing Runs Interceptions: Normal Interceptions Positioning Freedom: Stick to Position Defensive Position: Cover Centre

Position	Instructions
CAM	Defensive Support: Basic Defence Support Support on Crosses: Get into the Box for Cross Positioning Freedom: Stick to Position Interceptions: Normal Interceptions
Left ST	Support Runs: Stay Central Attacking Runs: Get in Behind Interceptions: Normal Interceptions Defensive Support: Basic Defence Support or Stay Forward
Right ST	Support Runs: Stay Central Attacking Runs: Get in Behind Interceptions: Normal Interceptions Defensive Support: Basic Defence Support or Stay Forward

4-3-2-1

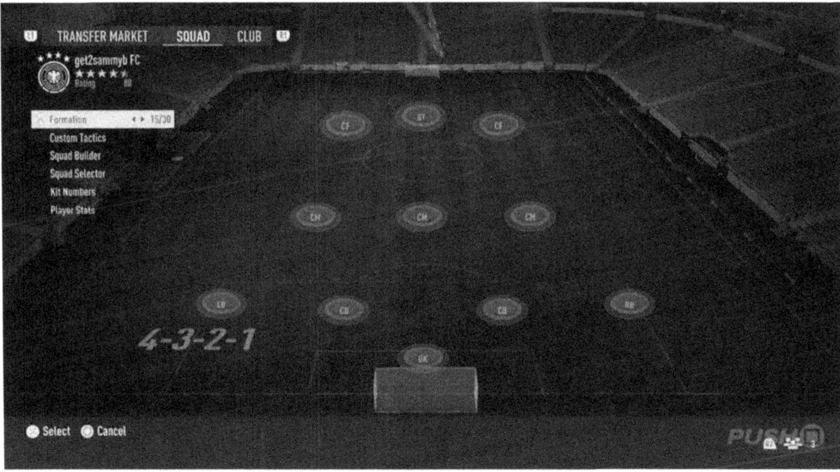

Formation	Pros	Cons
4-3-2-1	Tons of attacking options, with CFs supporting the lone striker and midfielders coming from deep. A compact formation that can be difficult for opponents to break down in front of goal.	Width relies on fullbacks getting forward where possible. Can be exposed by counter attacks and midfield can get stranded.

As mentioned above, the 4-3-2-1 is an attacking alternative to the 4-3-1-2, but it works well in FIFA 23, by providing you with a steady defensive structure and plenty of forwards you can use to build attacks around. The best way to play this formation is to keep it quite compact both defensively and offensively, meaning you're going to be working quite narrow. This means you will ultimately cede a lot of possession in wide areas, but you'll make up for this by being incredibly difficult to break down in front of goal.

Similarly, when you pick up possession, you're going to have a ton of options as you move the ball up the field, thanks to the sheer number of forwards and midfielders you have available. It can be quite easy to tap it around 4-4-2 formations as you'll almost always have extra options in the middle of the park, and if you want to be extremely aggressive you can push your fullbacks up to provide additional width. However, you must be wary of the counter-attack as it's easy to get exposed if your left back and right back are stranded upfield.

You can fiddle about with a 4-3-1-2 here and fluidly transition between the two as the situation arises, and even switch to a 4-3-3 to open up the pitch. Toggling between these, depending on what your opponent is doing, will make you quite difficult to predict, and therefore should lead to more opportunities as your opponent gets to grips with your rotating setups.

4-3-2-1 Custom Tactics

For your 4-3-2-1 Custom Tactics, you're ideally going to want to play quite narrow to keep the pitch nice and compact. Depending on how you play, you could go with an even narrower Width in Defence, as this will cause your fullbacks to really tuck in, making it difficult for opponents to find space in front of goal. Just be aware that you will be sacrificing wide positions this way, which could result in a number of crosses coming into the box. Make sure your central defenders are tall and physical, otherwise you may find yourself bullied by a big forward.

With regards to Build Up Play, we reckon that Balanced works best with Direct Passing here, as you have so many options moving through midfield and into the forward positions that you can really knock it around.

Fast Build Up is also a decent alternative option you could experiment with, depending on your own personal playstyle.

One thing you can do with your fullbacks is to assign one to get forward in attacking scenarios, while the other one stays back.

You're always going to have your CMs to help out in defence if you do get caught out, and we'd recommend that you use the most defensively minded of the trio as a CDM to Stay Back While Attacking and shuttle back and forth between the back four:

Defence

Defensive Style: Balanced

Width: 40

Depth: 50

Offence

Build Up Play: Balanced

Chance Creation: Direct Passing

Width: 40

Players in Box: 5

Corners: 1

Free Kicks: 1

We've included some example Instructions below, which should help to give you an idea of how to setup your Custom Tactics for the 4-3-2-1 formation. Tinker with these and find the optimal balance between offence and defence that works for you:

Position	Instructions
GK	Saving on Crosses: Balanced Saving Outside Box: Balanced
LB	Attacking Runs: Balanced Attack or Stay Back While Attacking Interceptions: Normal Interceptions Run Type: Mixed Attack Defensive Position: Stick to Position
Left CB	Attacking Support: Stay Back While Attacking Interceptions: Normal Interceptions Defensive Position: Stick to Position
Right CB	Attacking Support: Stay Back While Attacking Interceptions: Normal Interceptions Defensive Position: Stick to Position
RB	Attacking Runs: Balanced Attack or Stay Back While Attacking Interceptions: Normal Interceptions Run Type: Mixed Attack Defensive Position: Stick to Position
Left CM	Attacking Support: Balanced Attack or Get Forward Support on Crosses: Balanced Crossing Runs Interceptions: Normal Interceptions Positioning Freedom: Stick to Position

Position	Instructions
	Defensive Position: Cover Wing
Centre CM	Attacking Support: Stay Back While Attacking
	Support on Crosses: Balanced Crossing Runs
	Interceptions: Normal Interceptions
	Positioning Freedom: Stick to Position
	Defensive Position: Cover Centre
Right CM	Attacking Support: Balanced Attack or Get Forward
	Support on Crosses: Balanced Crossing Runs
	Interceptions: Normal Interceptions
	Positioning Freedom: Stick to Position
	Defensive Position: Cover Wing
LF	Support Runs: Stay Central
	Attacking Runs: Mixed Attack
	Interceptions: Normal Interceptions
	Defensive Support: Basic Defence Support
ST	Support Runs: Balanced Width
	Attacking Runs: Mixed Attack
	Interceptions: Normal Interceptions
	Defensive Support: Stay Forward
RF	Support Runs: Stay Central

Position	Instructions
	Attacking Runs: Mixed Attack
	Interceptions: Normal Interceptions
	Defensive Support: Basic Defence Support

3-1-4-2

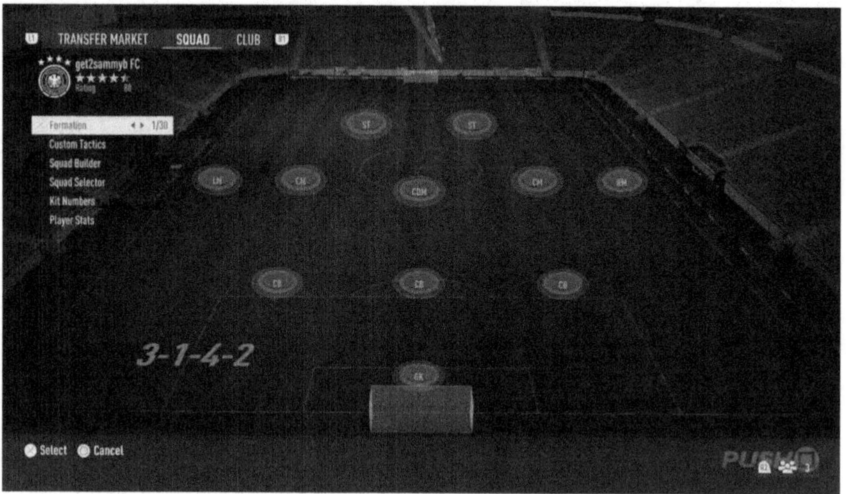

Formation	Pros	Cons
3-1-4-2	Versatile formation that can be offensive or defensive depending on the needs of your team. Plenty of defensive coverage, with a CDM always available to sniff out any potential counter-attacks.	Huge workload for wide midfielders can leave wings exposed. Forwards isolated if midfielders don't push up field to support.

The great thing about the 3-1-4-2 is that you can set it up to be both defensive or offensive depending on what your situation demands. For example, if you're chasing a goal then you can push your wingers high up the pitch, creating overloads in attack while still having the defensive coverage in midfield to not give away any easy goals. If you've got tall, powerful strikers then this can be particularly effective, as the wide midfielders will be able to cross into the box for them to finish.

On the flip-side, if you've got a lead that you need to cling on to in the latter stages of a game, then you can use your wide midfielders to assist in defence. While this will come at the expense of width, it'll make it extremely challenging for opponents to break you down, especially with the defensive midfielder shuttling backwards and forwards in front of your backline.

You could also consider using a 3-4-1-2 here, which functions in much the same way as the 3-1-4-2 but replaces the CDM with a playmaking CAM to help feed your forwards. Obviously, this comes at the expense of some defensive stability, but will make you more potent on the attack, especially if you prefer to play a possession-based game in midfield with pacey forwards making runs into space upfront.

3-1-4-2 Custom Tactics and Instructions

As mentioned previously, the 3-1-4-2 can be setup either offensively or defensively, but whatever you choose to do it's going to result in enormous workload for your wide midfielders. Unless you're chasing a goal late in a game, you're going to need them to Come Back on Defence because otherwise you're going to leave your wings wide open and exposed. Similarly, though, you're going to want them to join the attack if possible, and to even Get in Behind during offensive possessions. You need the right Players for this formation to function, because the workload is immense.

Fortunately, you have a ton of cover in midfield to help out should things go south. We'd recommend you set the Defensive Position of your Left CM and Right CM to Cover Wing, meaning they'll help out wide if your wingers get caught out. Meanwhile, you want your CDM to remain Cover Centre, to give some support and security in front of your backline.

You'll need to use a bit of Width here because this formation can easily get congested if you don't. We'd also recommend you use Long Ball as your Build Up Play tactic, as you can fling it up to your forwards and then win second balls from midfield. We've included some Custom Tactics below for you to tinker with as you feel necessary:

Defence

Defensive Style: Balanced

Width: 65

Depth: 50

Offence

Build Up Play: Long Ball

Chance Creation: Balanced

Width: 65

Players in Box: 5

Corners: 2

Free Kicks: 2

To build on this we've included some example Instructions for the 3-1-4-2 below. As always, you should tinker with this as you see fit. There's a lot of work for your LM and RM to do in this setup, so picking the right Players is critical here. It's a good idea to have a couple of substitutes in the same position who can deputise for your starters if they run out of gas:

Position	Instructions
GK	Saving on Crosses: Balanced Saving Outside Box: Balanced
Left CB	Attacking Support: Stay Back While Attacking Interceptions: Normal Interceptions Defensive Position: Stick to Position
Centre CB	Attacking Support: Stay Back While Attacking Interceptions: Normal Interceptions

Position	Instructions
	Defensive Position: Stick to Position
Right CB	Attacking Support: Stay Back While Attacking
	Interceptions: Normal Interceptions
	Defensive Position: Stick to Position
	Defensive Support: Come Back on Defence
	Chance Creation: Balanced Width
LM	Support Runs: Get in Behind
	Support on Crosses: Balanced Crossing Runs
	Interceptions: Normal Interceptions
	Attacking Support: Balanced Attack
	Support on Crosses: Balanced Crossing Runs
Left CM	Interceptions: Normal Interceptions
	Positioning Freedom: Stick to Position
	Defensive Position: Cover Wing
	Defensive Behaviour: Balanced Defence or Man Mark
	Attacking Support: Stay Back While Attacking
CDM	Interceptions: Normal Interceptions
	Defensive Position: Cover Centre
	Positioning Freedom: Stick to Position
Right CM	Attacking Support: Balanced Attack

Position	Instructions
	Support on Crosses: Balanced Crossing Runs
	Interceptions: Normal Interceptions
	Positioning Freedom: Stick to Position
	Defensive Position: Cover Wing
RM	Defensive Support: Come Back on Defence
	Chance Creation: Balanced Width
	Support Runs: Get in Behind
	Support on Crosses: Balanced Crossing Runs
	Interceptions: Normal Interceptions
Left ST	Support Runs: Stay Central
	Attacking Runs: Get in Behind
	Interceptions: Normal Interceptions
	Defensive Support: Stay Forward
Right ST	Support Runs: Stay Central
	Attacking Runs: Get in Behind
	Interceptions: Normal Interceptions
	Defensive Support: Stay Forward

FIFA 23: All Custom Tactics for FUT

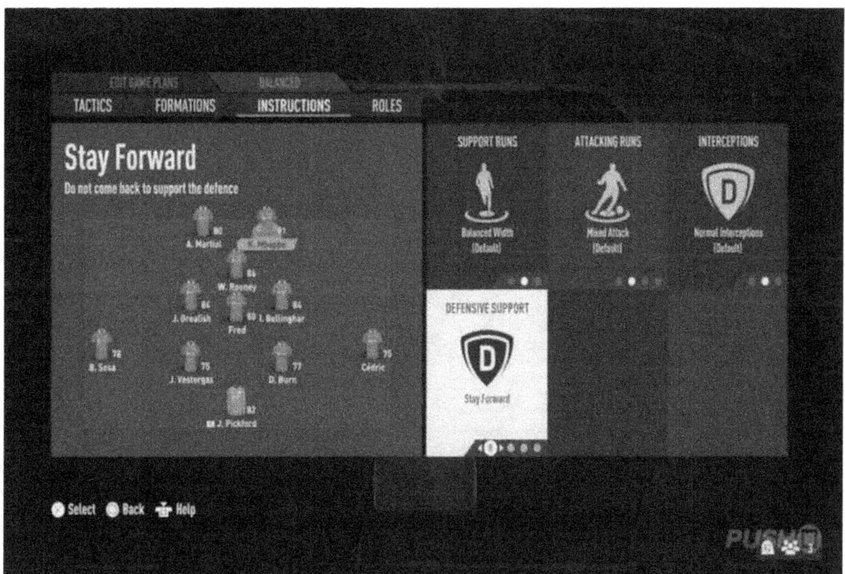

Deciding on the best formations for FUT is just one piece of the puzzle when building a formidable FUT 23 team: you'll also want to choose the best Custom Tactics for FUT as well. For all of the formations included above, we've provided example Custom Tactics, including Instructions, but none of these should be considered definitive. This is because a lot of what you select here will depend on your Players and what you're trying to achieve on the pitch. Many formations can become either offensive or defensive with just a few small adjustments.

Remember that you can create different Game Plans to suit an enormous variety of different scenarios, and you can change these mid-match by pushing left or right on the d-pad. If you're not sure what kind of Custom Tactics to employ for your formation, then we'd recommend you start out by keeping everything at its default settings. You can then hop into Squad Battles and start tinkering from there. For example, if you find that you're getting exposed in wide areas then you may want to consider adjusting your fullbacks' Attacking Runs instruction to Stay Back While Attacking. As you tinker, you'll begin to get a feel for the kind of Custom Tactics you want to leverage for your team.

If you're unsure of what the various Custom Tactics attributes actually do, then we've included a little more information for your reference below.

Defensive Tactics

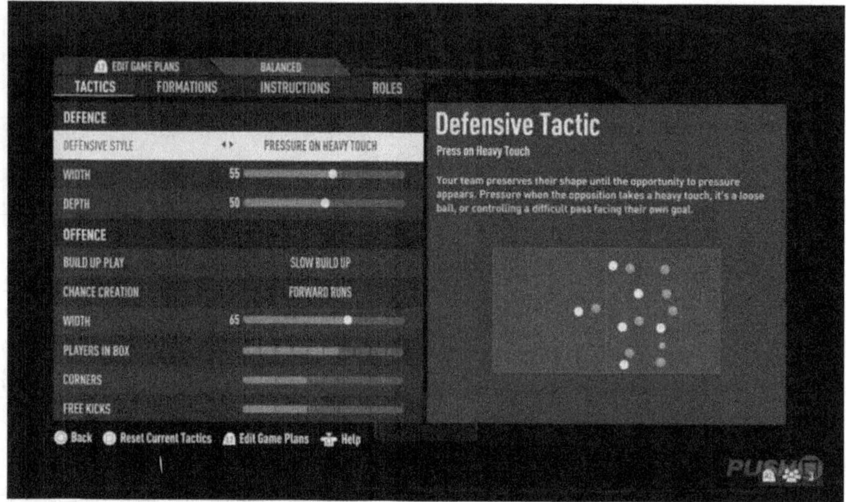

Defensive Tactics, unsurprisingly, refers to your team's shape when your opponent has possession of the ball. This determines how your team tries to win back possession, and how your team works to prevent the opponent from scoring.

Defensive Style

Balanced: Your team will adopt a neutral shape, without really pressing the opponent or dropping too deep.

Pressure on Heavy Touch: Your team will attempt to predict when the opponent is about to make a mistake, and will then quickly close them down to capitalise on the error and quickly win the ball back.

Press After Possession Loss: For seven seconds after losing the ball, your team will press the opponent hard in an attempt to win the ball back quickly. While this is powerful, it does come at the cost of significant stamina drain.

Constant Pressure: Similarly to Press After Possession Loss, this will put your players on a rampage to regain possession. It'll significantly drain stamina, and isn't really recommended unless you're chasing the game.

Drop Back: Your team will fall into a low block, ceding possession to your opponent but preventing them from threading the ball in behind you.

Width

Width: Refers to how spread or compact your players are when out of possession. We'd recommend keeping this quite neutral.

Depth

Depth: Refers to where your players sit on the pitch when out of possession.

Offensive Tactics

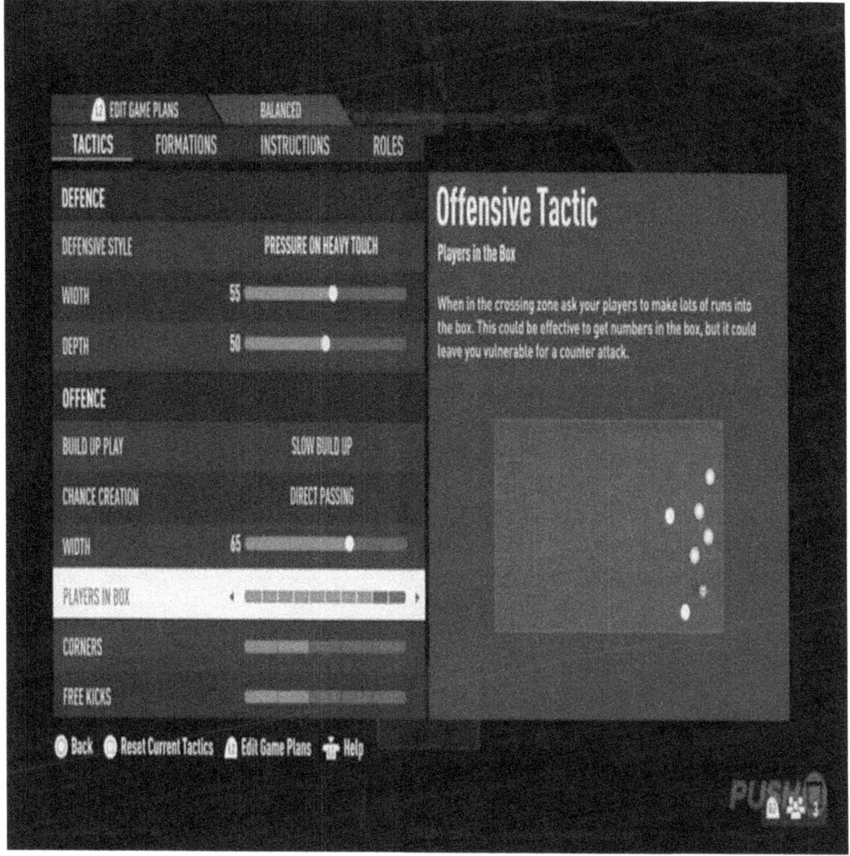

Offensive Tactics refers to how your team operates in possession. This includes how you build out from the back, and the approach your attackers take when outside your opponent's box. You settings here will determine how you penetrate your opposition's defence, and ultimately score goals.

Build Up Play

Balanced: Your team will adopt a combination of all the different Build Up Play styles, allowing you to mix up your approach as you feel necessary.

Fast Build Up: Your teammates will break forward at pace, allowing you to get the ball forward at pace but potentially leaving you open to counterattacks if you lose possession along the way.

Slow Build Up: Your teammates will come short and show for the ball allowing you to slowly build up possession from the back and move through the thirds of the pitch. Attackers will generally face up and show for the ball, as opposed to making incisive runs in behind.

Long Ball: Useful if you have a large target man who can lead the line and who you can hoof the ball up to.

Chance Creation

Balanced: Your teammates will hold their position when in the attacking third, making penetrating runs in behind either when you trigger them with L1 or when they feel it's the right time to do so.

Possession: A good complement for Slow Build Up if you're a possession based player, your teammates will show short and look for the ball rather than running in-behind through the defensive lines.

Forward Runs: Your teammates will look to penetrate the defence and get in-behind, at the expense of potentially being caught out if you lose possession during the build-up.

Direct Passing: Rather than necessarily in behind, your teammates will try to pull the defence out of position by running into areas of space and looking for the ball. This works well if you have a pacey team capable of dragging defenders around.

Width

Width: Refers to how spread or compact your players are when you have possession of the ball. If you're looking to spread the play then you'll want to bump this up, whereas if you want to be quite compact and play through the middle then you can move it down.

Players in Box

Players in Box: Refers to how many players run into the box when you get into crossing situations. This can leave you open to the counter attack if you push too many players forward and subsequently cede possession.

Corners

Corners: Refers to how many players enter the box during corners. A higher number here can leave you open to the counter attack if you lose possession during the set-piece.

Free Kicks

Free Kicks: Similar to Corners, this refers to how many players get in the box during free kicks and set-piece scenarios.

Again, it can leave you open to the counter attack if you select and high number here and subsequently lose possession.

FIFA 23: How to Make Coins Fast in FUT

Looking for how to make Coins fast in FUT in FIFA 23? Coins are a crucial in-game currency that you'll need in order to build your squad in FUT 23, which is also known as FIFA Ultimate Team.

You'll earn a small amount of Coins for every match that you play in FUT 23, regardless of whether you win or lose. However, in order to sign some of the best Players in the game, you're going to need a lot of Coins.

 On this page:

FIFA 23: How to Make Coins Fast in FUT

Play Plenty of Matches

Spend Time with Squad Battles and Division Rivals

Snipe Players from the Transfer Market

Sell Players You Don't Need

Pay Attention to SBCs

Don't Buy Gold Packs

Remember Your Managers, Consumables, and More

FIFA 23: How to Make Coins Fast in FUT

Once you've settled on the Best Formations and Custom Tactics for FUT, then you're going to want to fill it with the best Players in the game. Unfortunately, you're going to need to know how to make Coins fast in FUT in order to do that, whether it's buying players from the Transfer Market to go straight into your squad — or using them to complete Squad Building Challenges, or SBCs. On this page, as part of our FIFA 23 guide, we're going to share some strategies that should help you to learn how to make Coins in FUT.

Play Plenty of Matches

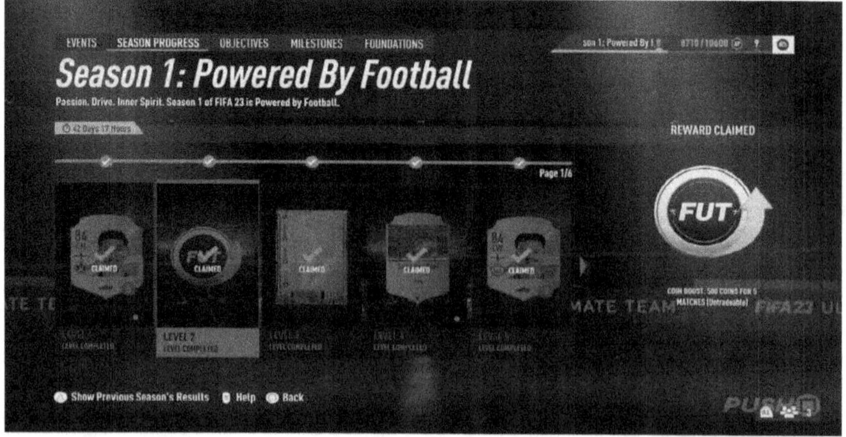

Look, it may sound stupidly obvious, but in order to easily
accumulate Coins you're going to want to make sure you're actually playing the
game. You'll get rewarded a bunch of Coins at the end of each match depending
on your performance, and this can add up surprisingly quickly and really
supplement your income. You'll unlock Coin Boosts as you progress
through Season Progress and Milestones which will increase the amount
of Coins you make.

Spend Time with Squad Battles and Division Rivals

Honestly, one of the easiest habits you can adopt that will help you with how to
make coins in FUT is to play plenty of Squad Battles and Division Rivals matches
every week. In the case of the former, you'll accumulate points for winning —
and even losing matches — every seven days, and these will help you to reach
different rewards tiers. The higher you rise through the ranks, the better your
rewards will be at the end. You can choose between Coins, Packs, or a mixture of
the two. Remember, if you plan to flip Players on the Transfer Market then you'll
want to make sure you avoid Untradeable packs, as you won't be able to sell
these. You will be able to use them in SBCs, however, which you should be
completing where desirable to remove the fodder from your card collection.

Snipe Players from the Transfer Market

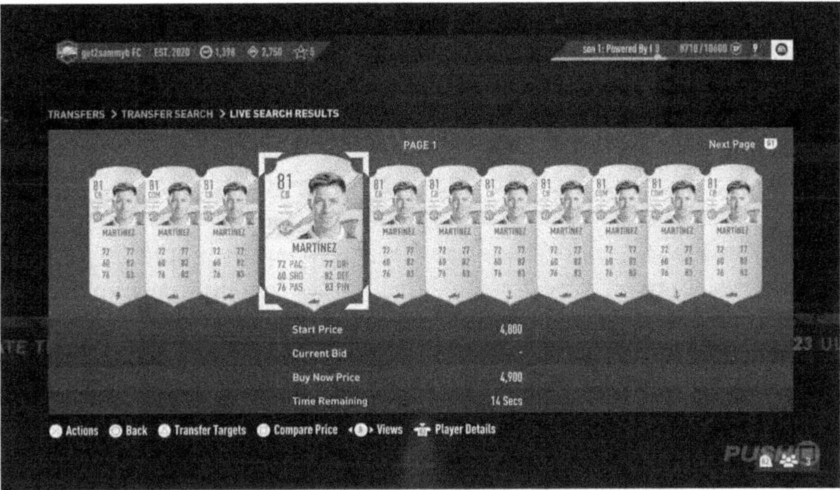

The Transfer Market is not just a great place to improve your team: it's also one
of the best destinations to make Coins. If you keep an eye on the Transfer

Market — either in-game, on the Web App, or on the smartphone Companion App — you will occasionally discover players selling for significantly less than their value. If the auction is close to concluding, you can try your luck and lodge a bid. While you won't always be successful, securing a card with an average selling price of 100,000 Coins for, say, 50,000 Coins is a huge win. You can then flip the player to make an enormous profit. You can usually get the best Transfer Market prices late at night on Sunday through until early in the morning on Monday. You should sell at any time from Thursday evening to Friday morning, as this period will traditionally fetch the highest prices during peak hours. For more information on When to Buy and Sell Players in FUT, click through the link.

Sell Players You Don't Need

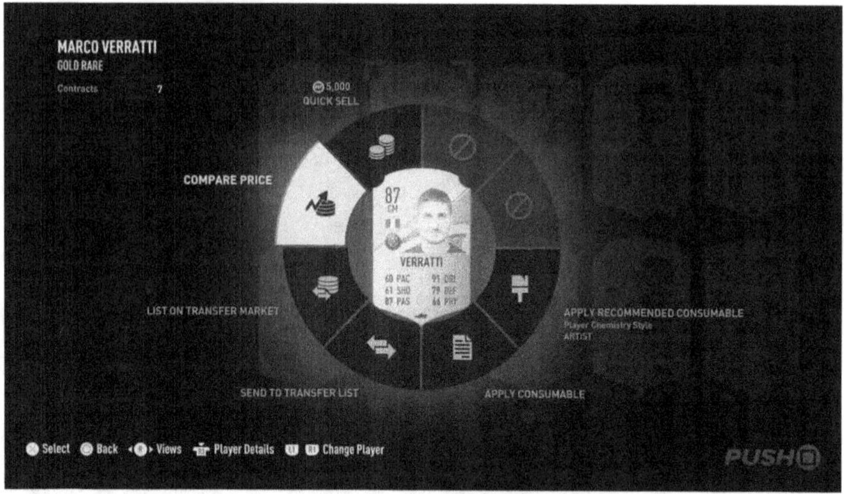

Depending on how active you intend to be with Squad Building Challenges, or SBCs, it's often a good idea to sell cards that you don't need. If you're lucky enough to pull a highly rated or meta Player, you can consider incorporating them into your team, or just cash in on them instead. Pay close attention to the average selling price of players on third-party websites, so you know their general value and don't get fleeced. We'd recommend exercising some patience and selling when prices are highest, usually on Thursday evenings through Friday mornings. While it can be tempting to open your Squad Battles rewards on Sunday morning and flip the Players you don't need right away, this is typically when selling prices are at their lowest, so just sit on the cards until later in the week and you'll make more Coins in the long-run.

Pay Attention to SBCs

Throughout the lifecycle of every FIFA game, EA Sports rolls out new time-limited SBCs or Squad Building Challenges. Whether you plan to complete these yourself or not, it can be a good idea to pay attention to the completion requirements, as this can affect the value of Players on the Transfer Market, including even low-value Players like Bronzes and Silvers. Team of the Week cards, or other promotional Players, can see a spike in value as fans rush to complete the latest SBCs, so sometimes it can be worth holding on to rare cards and flipping them at the appropriate moment. Try to pick peak hours to sell these Players, as if there are more people online trying to complete SBCs at the time, then this can help to drive up the value of your auctions.

Don't Buy Gold Packs

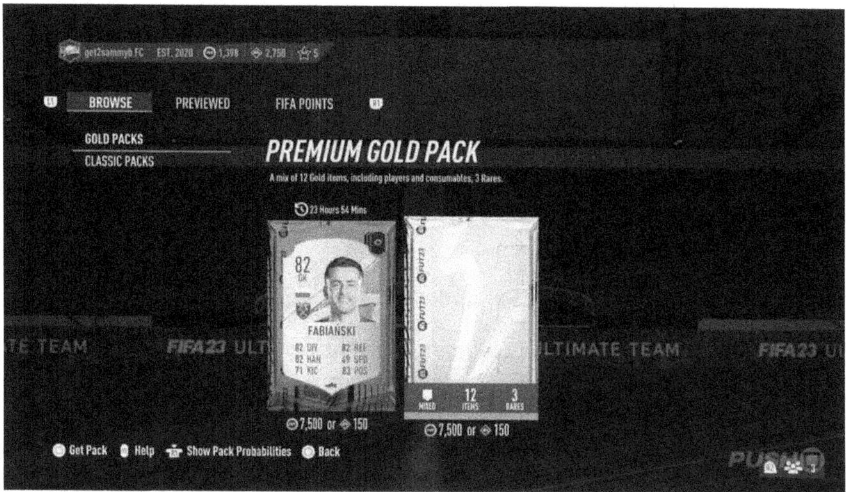

In FIFA 23, you can Preview one Gold Pack every 24 hours. You may as well do this because there's always a small chance that you'll pull something amazing, and you can effectively guarantee yourself a profit before you pod out. However, as a general rule, you really shouldn't be buying Gold Packs with your Coins. This is because, between Squad Battles, Division Rivals, Seasonal Milestones, and SBCs, there are loads of ways to earn packs. Furthermore, because these packs are so easy to earn, the Transfer Market is often flooded with Gold Players, driving down their overall value considerably. If you must buy packs with your Coins, then consider opting for Bronze Packs or Silver Packs instead. This is because there are fewer of these players on the Transfer Market, and therefore it's easier to profit on them — especially if you time your auctions to the release of SBCs. You can also use Bronze Players and Silver Players to complete Upgrade SBCs, which will help you earn enough fodder to complete the various Live promotional SBCs that roll out all year.

Remember Your Managers, Consumables, and More

When you're working the Transfer Market, it can be easy to forget about all the other items you pull from packs, whether it's Consumables like Chemistry or even Managers. Remember that Managers offer important boosts to teams based on their League, so are still a crucial component of the FUT 23 experience. This means that they have value, so if you have no use for certain gaffers, then flog them and get some easy Coins. Another thing to consider is buying players from the Transfer Market with the Chemistry Consumable you want already equipped. While this won't necessarily make you Coins, it will save you them, as you won't need to dive into the Transfer Market to buy the Consumables you want. Similarly, if you sell Players with a Chemistry Consumable attached, you can really increase your profit, especially if its a Shadow or Hunter item. Flogging off Cosmetics, like Kits and Stadium Items, won't earn you many Coins — but if you have a collection full of items you don't intend to use, it can add up quite quickly when you sell them off.

FIFA 23: How to Complete SBCs and Master Chemistry in FUT

Looking for how to complete SBCs and master Chemistry in FUT in FIFA 23? SBCs, also known as Squad Building Challenges, are a core part of the FUT 23 or FIFA Ultimate Team experience. In essence, they test your team building abilities by setting a variety of parameters which you'll need to fulfil in order to earn rewards.

 On this page:

FIFA 23: How to Complete SBCs and Master Chemistry in FUT

Dispose of Untradeable Players

Chemistry Explained

Make the Most of Upgrade SBCs

Use the Web App and Companion App

FIFA 23: How to Complete SBCs and Master Chemistry in FUT

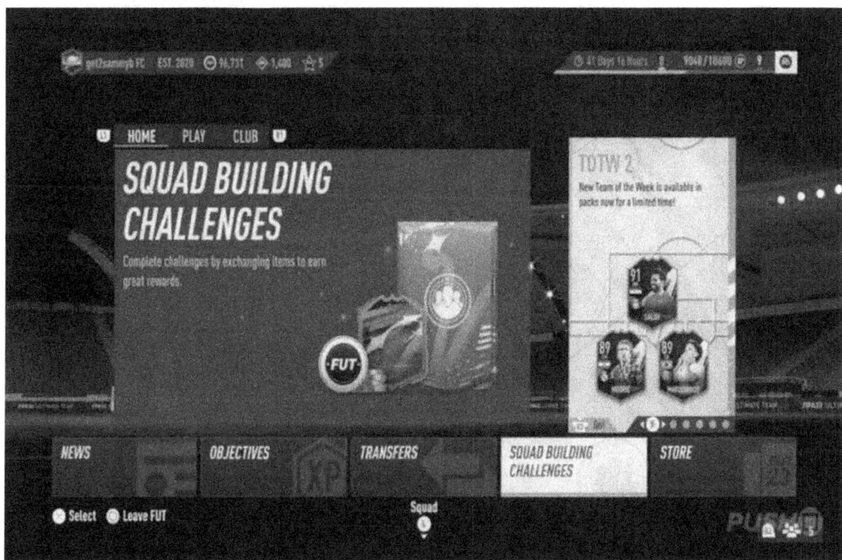

You'll collect a lot of Players in FIFA 23, and it's unlikely you'll use all of them for Division Rivals or FUT Champions. Instead, you'll either trade them on the Transfer Market or use them to complete SBCs, also known as Squad Building Challenges. Cards used primarily for SBCs are commonly referred to as "fodder" by the franchise's community, because they exist largely to fulfil the criteria of the team building challenges, as opposed to as starters in the Best Formations and Custom Tactics for FUT.

There are many SBCs available in FUT 23, and you'll find them in the Home section of the FIFA Ultimate Team main menu. If you're new to the game, then you should start by completing the SBCs listed under the Foundations tab. Not only are these extremely easy to complete, but you'll also get a number of free Packs for your troubles, which will help you to complete some of the other SBCs available in the game.

Below, as part of our FIFA 23 guide, we've included some suggestions which will help show you how to complete SBCs and master Chemistry in FUT. Remember that if you're struggling to complete an SBC or aren't sure how much an SBC will cost to complete, you can often find that information on third-party websites.

Dispose of Untradeable Players

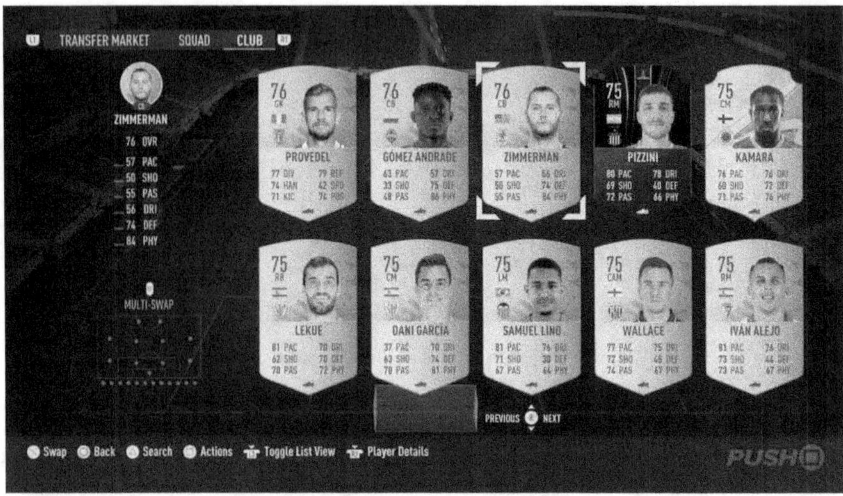

Some of the Players you'll collect as rewards for completing Seasonal
Objectives and Milestones will be Untradeable, which means they can't be traded
on the Transfer Market or Quick Sold. They can, however, be used to
complete SBCs. Always try to dispose of these cards when you can, especially if
you're not planning to use them in your team.

Chemistry Explained

Often you'll need to fulfil Chemistry requirements in order to complete SBCs. You
gain Chemistry by including players of the same Nationality, League, and Team.
The Chemistry system has changed in FIFA 23, allowing for a lot more flexibility in
team-building challenges.

In past FIFA games, players with similar attributes had to be connected
positionally in order to build Chemistry. For example, if you had two players with
the same Nationality and League in the CB position, you'd receive a Green
Chemistry link. However, in FIFA 23, Chemistry can be built across the entirety of
the pitch.

For example, if you have two English players in your team, they'll receive
one Chemistry block each, as long as they're in their designated position. Adding
three more English players to your team will award them all with
two Chemistry blocks each. However, you can also accrue Chemistry blocks by

choosing players from the same Team and League. A player can have
three Chemistry blocks each in total, meaning maximum Chemistry is reflected by
a team with 33 Chemistry. It's worth noting that in FIFA 23, players will always
perform at their base statistics, so Chemistry only ever provides bonuses and
never penalises you. You can also use your manager's League and Nationality to
add additional Chemistry blocks.

When it comes to SBCs, the best approach is to plan ahead. Think about the
requirements of the SBC you're trying to complete, and begin to
build Chemistry milestones so that you can comfortably fulfil the requirements of
the puzzle. Remember you can use Position Modifiers if you need to, although
we'd advise you don't waste these on SBCs if you can avoid it.

Make the Most of Upgrade SBCs

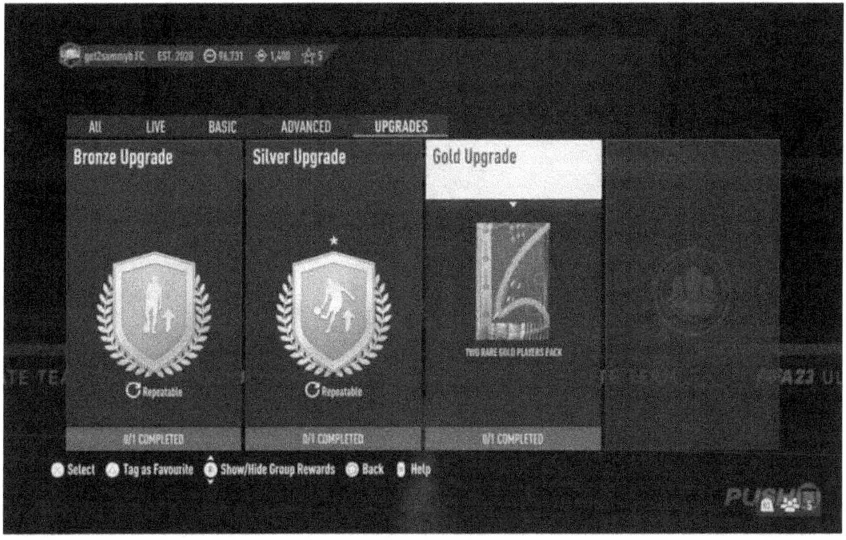

One easy method of How to Make Coins in FUT relies on you purchasing Bronze
Packs and using them to complete repeatable SBCs called Upgrades. First
complete the Bronze Upgrades to get Two Silver Players, then invest these
into Silver Upgrades to get Three Common Gold Players. You can then use
these Common Gold Players as fodder to help complete
promotional SBCs for Rare Players or Promo Packs. While it is, admittedly, a long-
winded and tedious process, if you're willing to put in the work you will get a lot
of high-quality Players for very little cost.

Use the Web App and Companion App

Chances are, when you've got FIFA 23 on your television, you're going to want to be playing matches of Division Rivals or FUT Champions. But by logging into your EA Sports account on your PC or smartphone, you can take advantage of the Companion App to complete SBCs while you're at work, on the bus, or even on the toilet. You can access the Web App through the link, and you'll find the Companion App on your smartphone's app store, on iPhone or Android.

Keep Useful Players in Your Club

If you pack a Team of the Week or other promotional player, it can be tempting to list them on the Transfer Market immediately. However, sometimes it can be valuable to keep these Players in your Club in anticipation of SBCs. Not only will their value increase as others seek out promotional cards in order to complete SBCs, but you may find that you're able to use them at a later date yourself in order to complete high value SBCs without needing to spend Coins.

What are all FUT Champions rewards, release dates, and times in FIFA 23? If you're playing FIFA Ultimate Team, also known as FUT 23, then you'll probably be familiar with FUT Champions, which is sometimes known as Weekend League. This is the pinnacle of FIFA Ultimate Team competition, requiring qualification through FUT Rivals. Unsurprisingly, then, the FUT Champions rewards are among some of the best in the game.

 On this page:

FIFA 23: FUT Champions - All Rewards, Release Dates, and Times

All FUT Champions Rewards

Champions Play Offs Rank 7

Champions Play Offs Rank 6

Champions Play Offs Rank 5

Champions Play Offs Rank 4

Champions Play Offs Rank 3

Champions Play Offs Rank 2

Champions Play Offs Rank 1

Champions Finals Rank 10

Champions Finals Rank 9

Champions Finals Rank 8

Champions Finals Rank 7

Champions Finals Rank 6

Champions Finals Rank 5

Champions Finals Rank 4

Champions Finals Rank 3

Champions Finals Rank 2

Champions Finals Rank 1

All FUT Champions Rewards Release Dates and Times

FIFA 23: FUT Champions - All Rewards, Release Dates, and Times

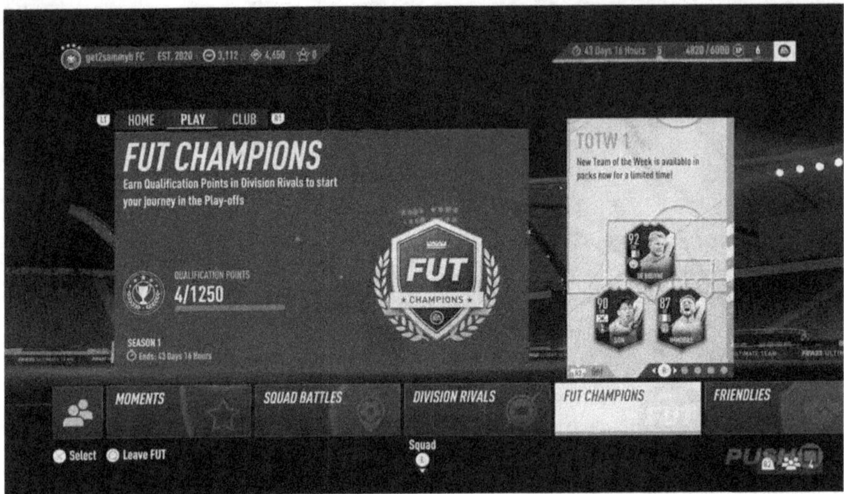

On this page, as part of our FIFA 23 guide, we're going to reveal all FUT Champions rewards, release dates, and times in FIFA 23. Please do note that FUT is a constantly evolving mode, and while we've endeavoured to keep the information on this page up-to-date, EA Sports could make changes at short notice rendering some information inaccurate.

All FUT Champions Rewards

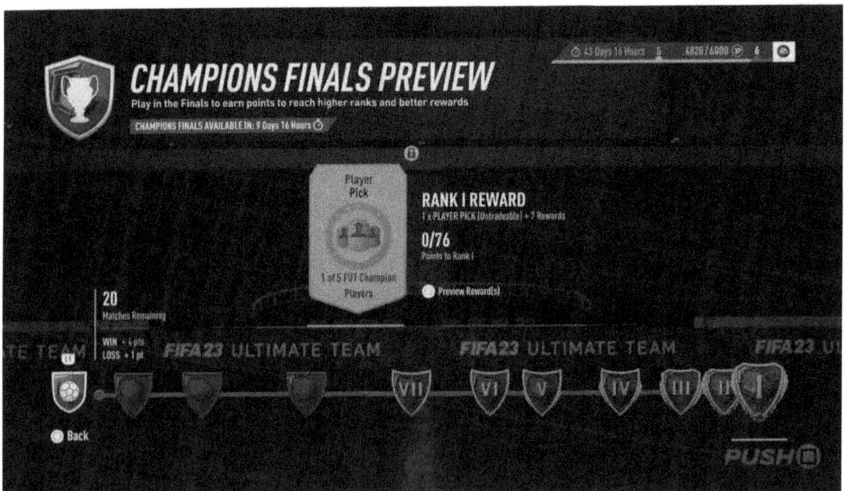

FUT Champions, also sometimes known as Weekend League, is similarly structured in FIFA 23 to FIFA 22. There are two phases to the FUT Champions competition: the Play Offs and the Finals. In order to participate in the FUT Champions Play Offs, you'll need to amass 1,500 FUT Champions Qualifications Points in FUT Rivals. Entry into the FUT Champions Finals requires you to reach Rank 2 in the FUT Champions Playoffs.

As soon as you've accrued enough FUT Champions Qualifications Points, you can play nine FUT Champions Play Off games whenever you like. You'll earn four points for a win and one point for a loss. If you reach at least Rank 2 then you'll qualify for the FUT Champions Finals, which must be played over a weekend period. You'll be able to play up to 20 matches in the FUT Champions Finals.

All FUT Champions rewards are listed below:

Champions Play Offs Rank 7

2 Jumbo Premium Gold Packs (Untradeable)

Champions Play Offs Rank 6

400 FUT Champions Qualification Points

2 Gold Players Packs (Tradeable)

1 Jumbo Premium Gold Pack (Tradeable)

Champions Play Offs Rank 5

Qualification to FUT Champions Finals

1 Small Prime Gold Players Pack (Tradeable)

2 Rare Gold Packs (Tradeable)

Champions Play Offs Rank 4

Qualification to FUT Champions Finals

1 Rare Gold Pack (Tradeable)

2 Mega Packs (Tradeable)

Champions Play Offs Rank 3

Qualification to FUT Champions Finals

2 Small Prime Gold Players Packs (Tradeable)

2 Rare Gold Packs (Tradeable)

1 Jumbo Premium Gold Players Pack (Tradeable)

Champions Play Offs Rank 2

Qualification to FUT Champions Finals

2 Small Rare Gold Players Packs (Tradeable)

1 Prime Gold Players Pack (Tradeable)

1 Rare Mega Pack (Tradeable)

Champions Play Offs Rank 1

Qualification to FUT Champions Finals

1 Mega Pack (Tradeable)

1 Rare Players Pack (Tradeable)

1 Jumbo Rare Players Pack (Tradeable)

Champions Finals Rank 10

500 FUT Champions Qualification Points

1 Rare Mixed Players Pack (Tradeable)

1 FUT Champion Players Pick (Untradeable)

Champions Finals Rank 9

500 FUT Champions Qualification Points

5,000 Coins

2 Jumbo Premium Gold Packs (Tradeable)

1 Prime Gold Players Pack (Tradeable)

1 FUT Champion Players Pick (Untradeable)

Champions Finals Rank 8

750 FUT Champions Qualification Points

10,000 Coins

2 Jumbo Premium Gold Packs (Tradeable)

1 Mega Pack (Tradeable)

1 Prime Gold Players Pack (Tradeable)

2 FUT Champion Players Picks (Untradeable)

Champions Finals Rank 7

750 FUT Champions Qualification Points

15,000 Coins

1 Rare Players Pack (Tradeable)

1 Jumbo Rare Players (Tradeable)

2 FUT Champion Players Picks (Untradeable)

Champions Finals Rank 6

1,000 FUT Champions Qualification Points

25,000 Coins

1 Premium Team of the Week Pack (Tradeable)

1 Rare Players Pack (Tradeable)

1 Jumbo Rare Players Pack (Tradeable)

2 FUT Champion Players Picks (Untradeable)

Champions Finals Rank 5

1,250 FUT Champions Qualification Points

30,000 Coins

1 Premium Team of the Week Pack (Tradeable)

1 Jumbo Rare Players Pack (Tradeable)

1 Ultimate Pack (Tradeable)

3 FUT Champion Players Picks (Untradeable)

Champions Finals Rank 4

1,250 FUT Champions Qualification Points

50,000 Coins

1 Premium Team of the Week Pack (Tradeable)

1 Jumbo Rare Players Pack (Tradeable)

1 Ultimate Pack (Tradeable)

3 FUT Champion Players Picks (Untradeable)

Champions Finals Rank 3

1,250 FUT Champions Qualification Points

75,000 Coins

2 Premium Team of the Week Packs (Tradeable)

2 Rare Players Packs (Tradeable)

1 Ultimate Pack (Tradeable)

3 FUT Champion Players Picks (Untradeable)

Champions Finals Rank 2

1,250 FUT Champions Qualification Points

100,000 Coins

2 Premium Team of the Week Packs (Tradeable)

2 Ultimate Packs (Tradeable)

3 FUT Champion Players Picks (Untradeable)

Champions Finals Rank 1

1,250 FUT Champions Qualification Points

100,000 Coins

3 Premium Team of the Week Packs (Tradeable)

1 Rare Players Packs (Tradeable)

2 Ultimate Packs (Tradeable)

3 FUT Champion Players Picks (Untradeable)

All FUT Champions Rewards Release Dates and Times

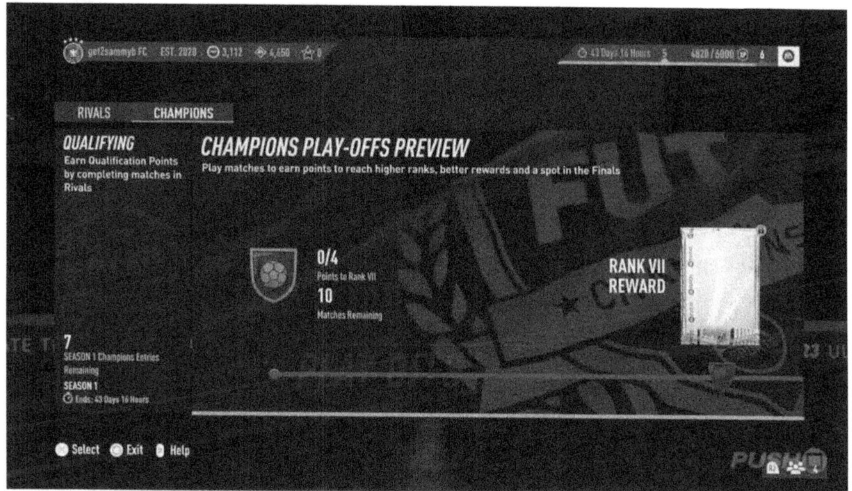

FIFA 23 Guide: Career Mode

For single player gamers, Career Mode is the holy grail of FIFA 23. Much like last year, you can take charge of a real-world club, but also create your own.
The Player Career has also been revamped, allowing you to develop your own on-field and off-field personality, as you work your way up to international glory. In this part of our FIFA 23 guide, we're going to help you find the Best Hidden Gems in Career Mode and much more.

All Starting Transfer Budgets in Career Mode

Best Hidden Gems in Career Mode

Highest Potential Players in Career Mode

FIFA 23: All Starting Transfer Budgets in Career Mode

What are all starting transfer budgets in Career Mode in FIFA 23? Starting transfer budgets are an important part of Career Mode, because some players like to begin their campaigns on a shoestring, while others prefer to work with flush clubs that can be active in the transfer market from the offset.

On this page:

FIFA 23: All Starting Transfer Budgets in Career Mode

England

Premier League

France

Ligue 1

Germany

Bundesliga

Spain

La Liga

FIFA 23: All Starting Transfer Budgets in Career Mode

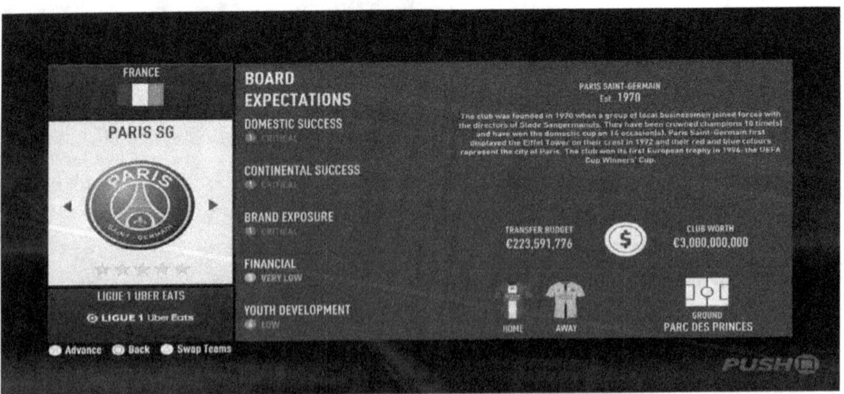

On this page, as part of our FIFA 23 guide, is a list of all starting transfer budgets in Career Mode in FIFA 23. Remember, if you want to receive an influx of cash at the beginning of your career, you can enable a Financial Takeover before starting your campaign. Nevertheless, we've listed the default starting transfer budgets below. We've divided the article by Nation and then League.

England

Premier League

Team	Pound Sterling
AFC Bournemouth	£27,279,488
Arsenal	£85,902,010
Aston Villa	£74,354,190
Brentford	£26,340,846
Brighton & Hove Albion	£42,092,490
Chelsea	£135,271,152
Crystal Palace	£42,219,149
Everton	£49,121,972
Fulham	£32,926,888
Leeds United	£44,393,534
Leicester City	£71,403,452

Team	Pound Sterling
Liverpool	£156,771,264
Manchester City	£233,750,920
Manchester United	£206,179,232
Newcastle United	£68,100,050
Nottingham Forest	£29,993,458
Southampton	£40,035,919
Tottenham Hotspur	£98,657,556
West Ham United	£62,643,032
Wolverhampton Wanderers	£56,813,124

France

Ligue 1

Team	Euro
AC Ajaccio	€7,552,615
AJ Auxerre	€9,255,060
Angers SCO	€11,314,020

Team	Euro
AS Monaco	€37,527,366
Clermont Foot	€7,817,299
Estac Troyes	€9,611,500
FC Lorient	€9,975,105
FC Nantes	€14,636,385
LOSC Lille	€22,314,390
Montpellier Hérault SC	€13,324,265
OGC Nice	€27,097,252
Olympique de Marseille	€34,196,462
Olympique Lyonnais	€51,583,476
Paris Saint-Germain	€223,591,776
Racing Club de Lens	€16,583,255
RC Strasbourg Alsace	€13,946,340
Stade Brestois 29	€11,767,980
Stade de Reims	€12,947,350

Team	Euro
Stade Rennais FC	€24,369,828
Toulouse FC	€9,988,799

Germany

Bundesliga

Team	Euro
1. FC Köln	€17,995,554
1. FSV Mainz 05	€16,472,389
Bayer Leverkusen	€68,577,008
Bayern München	€123,649,220
Borussia Dortmund	€80,807,396
Borussia Mönchengladbach	€31,393,522
Eintracht Frankfurt	€29,582,842
FC Augsburg	€19,002,545
FC Schalke 04	€22,611,400
Hertha Berlin	€42,834,948

Team	Euro
RB Leipzig	€83,658,376
SC Freiburg	€26,840,202
SV Werder Bremen	€15,813,937
TSG Hoffenheim	€43,746,550
Union Berlin	€20,008,154
VfB Stuttgart	€24,979,024
VfL Bochum	€11,976,850
VfL Wolfsburg	€52,817,790

Spain

La Liga

Team	Euro
Athletic Bilbao	€26,905,748
Atlético Madrid	€88,336,540
CA Osasuna	€13,800,576

Team	Euro
Cádiz	€11,751,320
Elche CF	€8,181,360
FC Barcelona	€162,502,712
Getafe CF	€16,640,036
Girona FC	€10,221,148
Real Valladolid CF	€10,696,250
Rayo Vallecano	€9,914,539
RC Celta de Vigo	€18,372,474
RCD Espanyol de Barcelona	€11,428,020
RCD Mallorca	€11,463,644

Team	Euro
Real Betis	€24,296,553
Real Madrid	€219,056,912
Real Sociedad	€25,497,973
Sevilla FC	€45,783,416
UD Almeria	€16,739,501
Valencia CF	€67,267,188
Villareal CF	€43,937,826

FIFA 23: Best Hidden Gems in Career Mode

Looking for the best hidden gems in Career Mode in FIFA 23? If you're looking to build a dynasty, either with your favourite team or a club you've created, then you're going to want to fill it with talent. Signing the likes of Lionel Messi and Cristiano Ronaldo can give you a shortcut to success, but if you want to sustain your rein, then you're going to want to pick up players with the potential to grow from a much younger age.

On this page:

FIFA 23: Best Hidden Gems in Career Mode

FIFA 23: Best Hidden Gems in Career Mode

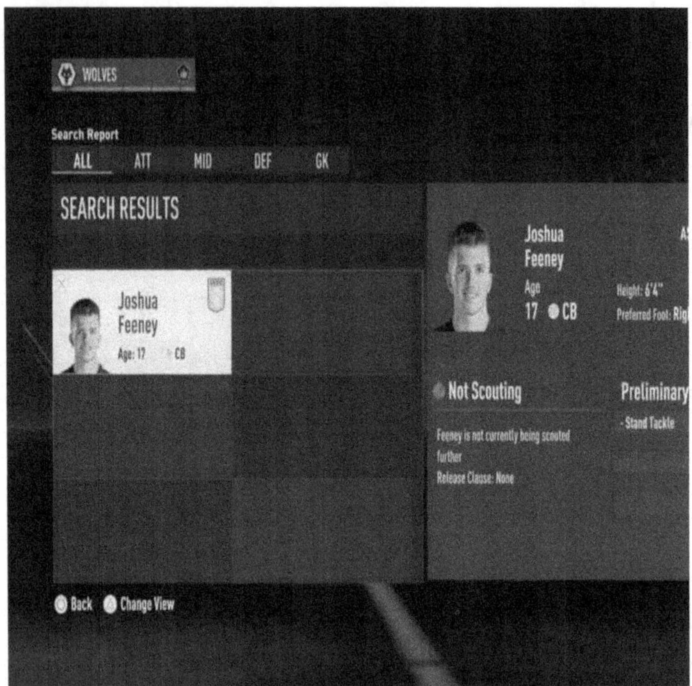

On this page, as part of our FIFA 23 guide, we've listed the best hidden gems in Career Mode in FIFA 23. We're ordering this list by Total Growth, which is calculated by subtracting their current OVR from their Potential. Essentially, with this list you're looking at players who are currently quite low-rated but have the Potential to become stars. As a result, you may be able to secure their services with relatively low transfer fees, making them great targets your team. If you're looking for a list of the highest potential players in Career Mode — and not necessarily Total Growth, as depicted below — then you can find that through the link.

Name	Team	League	Position	OVR	Potential	Total Growth
Joshua Feeney	Aston Villa	Premier League	CB	55	80	25
Felipe Valencia	Inter Miami	MLS	RM	50	75	25
Dylan Reid	St Mirren	Scottish Premiership	CDM	54	78	24
Diogo Monteiro	Servette FC	Swiss Super League	CB	54	78	24
Gavin Beavers	Real Salt Lake	MLS	GK	52	76	24
Attilio Morosoli	FC Lugano	Swiss Super League	GK	51	75	24
Andreș Brînzea	Chindia Târgoviște	SuperLiga României	GK	48	72	24
Luke Harris	Fulham	Premier League	CAM	61	84	23
Laurin Ulrich	VfB Stuttgart	Bundesliga	CM	60	83	23

Name	Team	League	Position	OVR	Potential	Total Growth
Cristian Riquelme	Everton de Viña del Mar	CONMEBOL Sudamericana	LB	60	83	23
Fabio Chiarodia	Werder Bremen	Bundesliga	CB	60	83	23
Alfie Devine	Tottenham Hotspur	Premier League	CAM	60	83	23
Arnaud Dony	Union Saint-Gilloise	Belgian Pro League	LB	59	82	23
Ashley Phillips	Blackburn Rovers	Championship	CB	59	82	23
Guillaume Restes	Toulouse FC	Ligue 1	GK	58	81	23
Ben Chrisene	Kilmarnock	Scottish Premiership	LB	58	81	23
Darko Gyabi	Leeds United	Championship	CM	57	80	23

Name	Team	League	Position	OVR	Potential	Total Growth
Serge Ngoma	New York Red Bulls	MLS	RW	56	79	23
Oliwier Sławiński	Zagłębie Lubin	Ekstraklasa	ST	54	77	23
Eirik Blikstad	Strømsgodset Toppfotball	Eliteserien	CB	54	77	23

FIFA 23: Highest Potential Players in Career Mode

Looking for the highest potential players in Career Mode in FIFA 23? You're going to need to break the bank to bring some of these emerging superstars to your club, but if you can tempt them to your team then you've got a guaranteed starter for up to a decade or more.

Many of these players already have stunning ratings to start with, but due to their young age and limitless ability, they have the potential to become future Ballon d'Or winners for sure.

 On this page:

FIFA 23: Highest Potential Players in Career Mode

On this page, as part of our FIFA 23 guide, we've listed the highest potential players in Career Mode in FIFA 23. We've ranked these players by Potential, but we've also included their current OVR so you know what you're getting. All of these players are under 24-years-old, so there's plenty of time for development. Please keep in mind that many of these players are on big contracts at their current clubs, however, so if you're looking for some budget stars of the future, check out the best hidden gems in Career Mode.

Name	Team	League	Position	OVR	Potential
Kylian Mbappé	PSG	Ligue 1	ST	91	95
Erling Haaland	Manchester City	Premier League	ST	88	94
Pedri	Barcelona	La Liga	CM	85	93
Phil Foden	Manchester City	Premier League	LW	85	92
Vinícius Jr	Real Madrid	La Liga	LW	86	92
Gianluigi Donnarumma	PSG	Ligue 1	GK	88	92
Florian Wirtz	Bayer Leverkusen	Bundesliga	CAM	82	91
Kai Havertz	Chelsea	Premier League	CAM	84	91

Name	Team	League	Position	OVR	Potential
Dušan Vlahović	Juventus	Serie A	ST	84	91
Jude Bellingham	Borussia Dortmund	Bundesliga	CM	84	91
Ansu Fati	Barcelona	La Liga	LW	79	90
Jamal Musiala	Bayern Munich	Bundesliga	CM	81	90
Rafael Leão	AC Milan	Serie A	LW	84	90
João Félix	Atletico Madrid	La Liga	SS	84	90
Sandro Tonali	AC Milan	Serie A	CDM	84	90
Alessandro Bastoni	Inter Milan	Serie A	CB	84	90
Trent Alexander-Arnold	Liverpool	Premier League	RB	87	90
Ryan Gravenberch	Bayern Munich	Bundesliga	CM	79	89
Eduardo Camavinga	Real Madrid	La Liga	CM	79	89

Name	Team	League	Position	OVR	Potential
Gavi	Barcelona	La Liga	CM	79	89
Vitinha	PSG	Ligue 1	CM	79	89

FIFA 23 Guide: Best Players

Whether you're eager to dominate against the CPU in Career Mode or blow away the pro players in FUT Champions, you're going to want to assemble the strongest squad possible. For the next part of our FIFA 23 guide, we're going to share our lists of the best players, helping you to better identify the superstars that will truly take your team to the next level.

All 5 Star Skill Players

Best Dribblers

Best Passers

Fastest Players

FIFA 23: All 5 Star Skill Players

Looking for all 5 Star Skill Players in FIFA 23? Whether you're looking to dominate FUT Champions or assemble a dream-team in Career Mode, you'll probably want to know which footballers are the most skilful in EA Sports' soccer sim. Fortunately, our FIFA 23 guide can help, and we've even pointed out the best Skill Moves to learn if you happen to have all 5 Star Skill Players in your squad.

 On this page:

FIFA 23: All 5 Star Skill Players

FIFA 23: All 5 Star Skill Players

On this page, you'll find a list of all 5 Star Skill Players in FIFA 23. We've ordered the players by their OVR rating, but you can use the table headings to adjust to your tastes. Also of interest, we've prepared a list of the Best Skill Moves to Learn.

Name	Team	League	Position	OVR	Skill Moves
Kylian Mbappé	PSG	Ligue 1	ST	91	
Cristiano Ronaldo	Manchester United	Premier League	ST	90	
Neymar Jr	PSG	Ligue 1	LW	89	
Vinícius Jr	Real Madrid	La Liga	LW	86	
Christopher Nkunku	RB Leipzig	Bundesliga	SS	86	
Kingsley Coman	Bayern Munich	Bundesliga	LM	86	
Thiago	Liverpool	Premier League	CM	86	
Riyad Mahrez	Manchester City	Premier League	RW	86	
Memphis Depay	Barcelona	La Liga	SS	85	
Paul Pogba	Juventus	Serie A	CM	85	
Jadon Sancho	Manchester United	Premier League	LW	84	

Name	Team	League	Position	OVR	Skill Moves
João Félix	Atletico Madrid	La Liga	SS	84	
Martin Ødegaard	Arsenal	Premier League	CAM	84	
Ángel Di María	Juventus	Serie A	RW	84	
Ousmane Dembélé	Barcelona	La Liga	RW	83	
Hakim Ziyech	Chelsea	Premier League	RW	83	
Roberto Firmino	Liverpool	Premier League	SS	83	
Juan Cuadrado	Juventus	Serie A	RB	83	
Antony	Manchester United	Premier League	RW	82	
Lucas Paquetá	West Ham United	Premier League	CAM	82	
Wilfried Zaha	Crystal Palace	Premier League	LW	82	

Name	Team	League	Position	OVR	Skill Moves
Coutinho	Aston Villa	Premier League	CAM	82	
Zlatan Ibrahimović	AC Milan	Serie A	ST	82	
Marcus Rashford	Manchester United	Premier League	LW	81	
Allan Saint-Maximin	Newcastle United	Premier League	LM	81	
Jesús Corona	Sevilla	La Liga	RW	81	
David Neres	Benfica	Primeira Liga	RW	79	
Jesper Karlsson	AZ	Eredivisie	LW	78	
Igor Coronado	Al Ittihad	Saudi Pro League	CAM	77	
Franck Ribéry	Salernitana	Serie A	SS	77	
Jota	Celtic	Scottish Premiership	LW	76	

Name	Team	League	Position	OVR	Skill Moves
Matheus Pereira	Al Hilal	Saudi Pro League	CAM	76	
Marcelino Moreno	Atlanta United	MLS	CAM	76	
Luciano Acosta	FC Cincinnati	MLS	CAM	76	
Xherdan Shaqiri	Chicago Fire	MLS	CAM	76	
Silas	VfB Stuttgart	Bundesliga	RM	75	
Amine Harit	Olympique de Marseille	Ligue 1	LM	75	
Daniel-Kofi Kyereh	SC Freiburg	Bundesliga	CAM	75	
Alexandru Maxim	Gaziantep FK	Süper Lig	CAM	75	
Cesinha	Daegu FC	K League 1	LW	75	
Rayan Cherki	Olympique Lyonnais	Ligue 1	LW	73	

Name	Team	League	Position	OVR	Skill Moves
Talles Magno	New York City FC	MLS	LM	71	
Hernâni	Rio Ave	Primeira Liga	RM	71	
Modou Barrow	Jeonbuk Hyundai Motors	K League 1	LM	70	
Juan Diego Rojas	Delfín SC	CONMEBOL Sudamericana	RM	68	
Osame Sahraoui	Vålerenga Fotball	Eliteserien	LW	67	
Aiden McGeady	Hibernian	Scottish Premiership	LM	67	
Dylan Bahamboula	Livingston	Scottish Premiership	RW	63	

FIFA 23: Best Dribblers

Looking for the best dribblers in FIFA 23? While there are many essential skills to master in EA Sports' soccer sim, you're going to want players who are good with the ball at their feet if you expect to succeed, regardless of whether you're playing FUT 23 or Career Mode. Fortunately, as part of our FIFA 23 guide, we're going to list the best dribblers you can add to your squad.

 On this page:

FIFA 23: Best Dribblers

FIFA 23: Best Dribblers

On this page, you'll find a list of the best dribblers in FIFA 23. We've ordered the players based on their DRI rating, but we've also included their OVR so you can get a snapshot of their overall ability.

Name	Team	League	Position	OVR	DRI
Lionel Messi	PSG	Ligue 1	RW	91	94
Neymar Jr	PSG	Ligue 1	LW	89	93
Kylian Mbappé	PSG	Ligue 1	ST	91	92
Bernardo Silva	Manchester City	Premier League	CAM	88	92
Marco Verratti	PSG	Ligue 1	CM	87	91
Vinícius Jr	Real Madrid	La Liga	LW	86	90

Name	Team	League	Position	OVR	DRI
Riyad Mahrez	Manchester City	Premier League	RW	86	90
Paulo Dybala	Roma	Serie A	SS	86	90
Mohamed Salah	Liverpool	Premier League	RW	90	90
Thiago	Liverpool	Premier League	CM	86	90
Jadon Sancho	Manchester United	Premier League	LW	84	89
Lorenzo Insigne	Toronto FC	MLS	LW	84	89
Allan Saint-Maximin	Newcastle United	Premier League	LM	81	88
Isco	Sevilla	La Liga	CAM	82	88
Mateo Kovačić	Chelsea	Premier League	CM	84	88
Christopher Nkunku	RB Leipzig	Bundesliga	SS	86	88
João Félix	Atletico Madrid	La Liga	SS	84	88

Name	Team	League	Position	OVR	DRI
Coutinho	Aston Villa	Premier League	CAM	82	88
Sadio Mané	Bayern Munich	Bundesliga	LM	89	88
Dries Mertens	Galatasaray	Süper Lig	SS	84	88

FIFA 23 Guide: Gameplay

It doesn't matter which mode of FIFA 23 you're playing, it's always a good idea to familiarise yourself with the basics and setup your game correctly. For this part of our FIFA 23 guide, we're going to focus on small details you can learn or settings you can tweak to become a beast on the pitch.

Best Controller Settings and Camera

Best Skill Moves to Learn

How to Do Power Shots

This FIFA 23 guide is a work in progress so be sure to check back for more information

FIFA 23: FAQs

For the penultimate section of our FIFA 23 guide, we're going to dig into the questions that haven't necessarily been answered anywhere else.

Release Dates - EA Play Trial and Ultimate Edition Early Access

FIFA 23 Guide: Tips and Tricks for How to Win More Matches

Whether you're playing Career Mode matches against the CPU or trying to reach the upper-echelons of FUT Rivals, the goal in FIFA 23 is learning how to win more matches. For the final part of our FIFA 23 guide, we're going to help you to master the pitch, and become an unstoppable force both online and offline.

Defending Tips: How to Concede Fewer Goals

If you want to know how to win more matches in FIFA 23, then a good place to start is by conceding fewer goals. It goes without saying that defending is the foundation upon which your results are built: if you don't concede any goals then the absolute worst result you can get is a draw. In this section of our FIFA 23 guide, we're going to share some defending tips that will hopefully help show you how to concede fewer goals:

A good place to start is to defend with midfielders whenever possible. If you're using a formation with CDMs, then select them with either the L1 button or the right analogue stick and use them to challenge attackers, block passing lanes, and track runners. The reason to do this is because it'll prevent you from stepping out of shape with your centre backs, allowing the AI to retain a robust defensive line. In most cases this will mean that even if your CDM is beaten, your centre backs will still be available to mop up any danger.

In most cases, you don't need a standing tackle or sliding tackle. The best way to defend is by staying on your feet and jockeying your opponent out wide with the L2 button. If you position your body correctly then you'll stab the ball away, but by not committing you'll also be able to block passing lanes and shepherd attackers away from the goal. Do not over commit as you will get beaten: play it cool, retain good defensive shape, and don't let your opponent catch you out of position. Try not to be too aggressive as you'll be picked off, so just focus on making it difficult for your opponent until they make a mistake.

If you can't stop the attacker from getting through on goal, then the best you can do is to minimise the risk of them scoring. If you know which players your opponent is using then try to force them onto their weaker foot, or at least shepherd them out wide. Limit your opponent to low-probability shots, like attempts outside of the box or with difficult angles. While you will, inevitably, concede plenty of goals over time, lowering the odds against you will at least put you in the best possible position to win.

Attacking Tips: How to Score More Goals

Of course, if you want to know how to win more matches then you're going to need to know how to score more goals. The brutal reality is that even if your defence is impenetrable, you're not going to win any matches if you can't score a goal. So, for the next phase of our FIFA 23 guide, we're going to share some attacking tips, which will hopefully help show you how to score more goals:

You can't score a goal if you don't have possession of the ball, so regardless of your tactics and approach, our first recommendation is to make sure you're recycling the ball when you have no obvious advantage. The best way to score is to pull your opponent out of position, but if you're up against a good player, there's a high probability that they won't bite. You need to keep moving and working the ball until an opportunity opens up. But it's important to remember that as long as the ball is in your possession, your opponent can't score. This keeps you on the front foot, and will inevitably lead to errors, which will be your best opportunity to strike.

While you don't need to become a total dribble merchant, it can be a good idea to learn a few skill moves. Manoeuvres like the fake shot — performed by pushing the shoot button followed by the pass button — can help you to beat opponents and gain a yard or two of space. This can be particularly effective when you're one-on-one against a rushing goalkeeper, as you can sit them down and shoot into an empty net. This increases your probability of scoring significantly, which is the outcome you obviously want.

Don't be afraid to switch the play and work the ball out wide. Crossing is pretty effective in FIFA 23, and something you'll want to take advantage of as opposed to just working the ball through the middle. If your formation allows it, make sure your wide players are getting into the box in crossing situations, so you have options at both the near post and far post to exploit.

The aerial game is much more potent this year, meaning that lofted through balls can be deadly in attack. Hold the L1 button and push triangle to lift the ball into space. You're going to want to put a little extra bite on the pass so you put it into the area ahead of your striker to run onto, rather than play it to feet.

General Tips: How to Keep Your Head

FIFA 23 is a highly competitive game that's brilliantly entertaining both in victory and defeat, but the very nature of the game means you will experience moments when you'll need to know how to keep your head. As part of our FIFA 23 guide, we're going to share some more general tips, which we hope will help keep you cool and show you how to keep your head:

Perhaps the most difficult but important thing to accept is that, frankly, there are other players who are better than you. This doesn't mean you should throw in the towel and call it a day: instead accept that you can improve at the game, and try to learn from what your opponents do. You don't have to be the number one player in the world to enjoy playing FIFA 23, so adopt an optimistic attitude and try your best. If you get beat, then you get beat. But ask yourself: why did you get beat? What did your opponent do differently? And what can you change to give yourself a better chance of victory next time?

Even though you will come up against better players at times in FIFA 23, there will also be occasions where you feel you should have won. We've all experienced it: a goalkeeping error, a penalty that should never have been awarded, or a deflection that trickles into the goal. It happens. If you feel your blood pressure increasing, then it's time to take a break. Remember that you're supposed to be playing the game to relax and have fun. If your mood is bad, then you'll inevitably make more mistakes, which will only compound your anger. So if you can't keep calm, then it's time to turn the game off entirely.